INTERSECTION
between slavery and
the military in Haiti

INTERSECTION
between slavery and the military in Haiti

JUSTICE AND PEACE ARE THE
RIGHT BALANCE OF POWER

Yonie Richard

iUniverse, Inc.
New York   Bloomington

Intersection between the Slavery and the Military in Haiti
Justice and Peace Are the Right Balance of Power

iUniverse books may be ordered through booksellers or by contacting:

iUniverse
1663 Liberty Drive
Bloomington, IN 47403
www.iuniverse.com
1-800-Authors (1-800-288-4677)

ISBN: 978-1-4401-6169-8 (pbk)
ISBN: 978-1-4401-6170-4 (ebk)

Printed in the United States of America

iUniverse rev. date: 9/10/2009

Contents

In the strictest sense, both slavery and the military in Haiti not only have a common intersection, but also a commutative reaction in which they are equal to each other. After studying the behavior of both slaves and soldiers, Haitian observers are finally discovering that they are the same. In fact, a slave is someone who is poorly educated and who we understand was sold by his own brothers to rich white people a long time ago. A person in the military is another slave, who is not only trained for specific reasons, but also who has accepted being a slave in uniform. Do you think that either of them knows what freedom looks like? They are inextricably linked to each other, and I don't believe anyone can probably talk about one without also addressing the others.

Slaves and the Military

Slaves and members of the military have broken spirits. The Bible gives us a message that is the answer to all forms of slavery since we must obey to the laws. In fact, we live in a world where slavery is still a reality. Looking at the problems Haiti has endured and what we Haitians, both within Haiti and abroad, have been doing, the solution is simple. We must sit down together and think about how to change our slave mentality to one of freedom and independence. We need to stop blaming others for our problems, and stop criticizing, killing, kidnapping, and raping others, especially our own citizens. In reality, with all of those problems, even though we have proclaimed our independence, we remain slaves.

Most notably, slavery and the military have developed the idea of the organized/disorganized dichotomy, in which they both have been divided by class and group. Both of them are suffering from this division, making it uncomfortable for them to live anywhere they happen to be. This dichotomy has psychologically impacted them to where they are not only having a hard time surviving, but they are unable to socialize with others. As a result of this, they have no peace, the flavor and enjoyment of life has vanished for them, and most of them become unhappy, violent, and criminal. In fact, "Organized crimes are premeditated and carefully planned, so little evidence is found at the scene. Organized criminals, according to the classification scheme, are antisocial but know right from wrong, are not insane, and show no remorse. Disorganized crimes, in contrast, are not planned, and criminals leave such evidence as fingerprints and blood. Disorganized criminals may be young, under the influence of alcohol or drugs, or mentally ill" (Winerman 2004).

Now, our Haitian children are in trouble in the streets! We are unable to understand that children's behaviors reflect adult behaviors. We are not satisfied with our political and economic gains, and we cannot seem to find ways to mobilize effective forces for corrective changes in order to rebuild black communities and families in Haiti.

Why do you, my fellow Haitians, blame the whites each time by thinking that they are against us? In reality, that is not fair for either group; all of us should remember the day when the blacks from Africa sold their own brothers and sisters for munitions. Today they are still continuing the same thing in Haiti, where they are even selling their own kids into prostitution in the Dominican Republic.

According to Father Pedro Ruquoy, who runs a refuge near Barahona: "There is a thriving trade in Haitian children in the Dominican Republic, where they are mostly used for domestic service, agricultural work, or prostitution? An eight-year-old boy was one of them. Numbed by a mixture of trauma and shyness, this small boy with huge eyes cannot recall how he left his three brothers and mother in Haiti and ended up doing domestic work for a Dominican family in Barahona, 120 miles from the capital, Santo Domingo" (Younge 2005).

Nobody knows quite how many Haitian children like him there are in the Dominican Republic. A UNICEF report in 2002 put the figure at around 2,500, although some NGOs think it might be twice that. Most boys under the age of twelve end up begging or shoe shining and giving their proceeds to gang leaders; most girls of that age are used as domestic servants. Older boys are taken to work in construction or agriculture; teenage girls often end up in prostitution. "They used him as a slave," says Mr. Ruquoy, "and they tortured him" (Younge 2005).

We are the ones who started this game in the beginning.In any business, there is a seller and a buyer, in fact, buyers do not know if there is a sale unless the sellers advertise which proves to everyone around the world that the slaves had sold themselves.

In a good sense, slavery has been one of the best adventures that has allowed you to achieve your creative, definitive plans in your life. Besides, would you have been able to accomplish anything more for yourself, if your ancestors had not been sold into slavery and were still living in Africa? If you were living in Africa today, your life would be harder there than it is in Haiti.

Since we fully understand the facts about slavery, it becomes easy to resolve them and put an end to it. The first step to solve any problems is to understand the root cause of the problem to be resolved. As soon as you have finally identified and overcome that particular aspect, the other problems will be able to resolve themselves.

Similarly, in the broader sense of the world, military service involves those voluntarily consigned to enslavement, but in general such slavery has an enduring, almost permanent, psychological defect. "Most of those men, regardless of race, who are serving their time, suffer from post-traumatic stress disorder (PTSD) a psychological reaction to extreme physical and emotional trauma" (U.S. Army 2007). The symptoms of PTSD are acute anxiety, depression, insomnia, irritability, flashbacks, numbing, and emotional and physical hyperalertness. Recent studies show that military mental disorders appear to be indicated not only by more chronic or severe diseases, but also by a variety of behavioral problems, such as misconduct, alcohol abuse, prostitution, and unprotected sex, leading to sexually transmitted diseases (STDs).

Generally speaking, most of those who have served in the military in Haiti have been those with poor birthrights or who had bad luck in society. As Aristotle declared about the history of slavery in Rome and Greece, "all of those barbarian men are considered to be slave birth, fit for nothing but obedience." In addition to this, he also mentioned that "barbarians arc slave by nature" (Aristotle 2000). We all know that the word *slavery* is used to describe a number of related conditions involving the control of persons against their will, enforced by violence and trickery. Based upon my experience, neither slaves nor soldiers have rights: the reason is that each must ask permission to do anything, and no one is allowed to move around without an executive order. Slave owners and military leaders enforce very strict regulations, making both realms similar.

Everyone is born with three things: talents, gifts, and power. Your thinking process determines success. It is definitely not as easy as it sounds, but some say, "Think rich, be rich." Therefore, we all have the potential to manifest and make our own reality, good or bad. The socioeconomic triangle has placed the poor at the bottom, then the lower middle class, middle class, upper middle class, and the wealthy, respectively. The triangle is topped by the wealthy, and there is one thing that they all have in common: somewhere in their lifetimes, the unique trait of discipline was instilled in them. Today, everyone needs self- discipline, wit, education, and book and street knowledge in order to succeed in a world that is full of lions, tigers, ligers, raccoons, rats, and snakes.

I have not even mentioned the importance of maintaining your religious aspects by keeping the Bible in mind. The two greatest commandments in Scripture are love God with all your heart and love your neighbor as yourself. He also said that no one has a right to murder or violate the freedom of another. My dear friends around the world, if we are murdering, raping, and kidnapping, it is simply because we do not respect our Creator.

Another cause may be that a chromosome in the embryo becomes defective. The reason we think this is the case is due to the rate of violence and crime, which is more overwhelming in our culture than any other race on earth. In fact, researchers have recently shown that men with a monoamine oxidase A deficiency (MAOA) are born with XYY syndrome, also called Jacob's Syndrome, and are taller, produce more testosterone, and are more violent than the men who are born with one Y chromosome. This makes it very complicated as to whether this particular case might influence antisocial behavior or criminal activity. "Early reports claim that the population of XYY men in prison is between ten and sixty times more than the general population" (Paul Aitken, 2007). Remarkably "about 1 in 1,000 newborn males are born with an X and two Y chromosomes, thereby creating the supermale" (Steen 1996, p. 232). "Within the last fifty years there have been many studies in most of the prisons between the XYY chromosome and criminal behavior." Based on the studies that suggested that, "1 in 1,000 men would indeed carry the extra Y chromosome, the scientists did not expect to find seven inmates with the chromosome abnormality. The unexpected results brought the percentage of the population of XYY males to 3.5" (Taylor 1984, p. 76).

Our fragmented efforts on governing and planting a democracy in Haiti are like small spider webs that are easily broken once the wind blows, not even waiting for a storm. We keep blaming the whites, who have little to do with our failures. The color of skin does not determine anyone's relevance on the social scale. Malcolm X, one of the slave brothers, pronounced about a slave that "he wants to make a life for himself where he is free to live as he pleases...He does not want to live under the boot heel of his abusive, jealous master" (Breitman 1965).

However, after studying the behavior of blacks from the full range of socioeconomic conditions, one thing is clear: many of us still act as if we internalize inferiority. Also, some who no longer live in the ghetto retain their ghetto mentality and often carry it wherever they go. In business, blacks run away from other blacks at the drop of a hat, even though they belong to the same social class, are members of the same professional organizations, or come from the same town. We are dying for other people's approval so badly that we refuse to embrace our own. Believe it or not, this self-imposed complex has caused more damage to our progress than anything in the history of racism. As long as we entertain such beliefs, we will never find a way out of this shadow of darkness to save the black families. The whites (especially the Americans) have nothing to do with it.

According to history, during times of slavery, slaves were tortured with three major mental problems: fear, distrust, and envy. That happened over two centuries ago. By way of example, if you copy an original document, then make a copy of that copy, and then continue copying the previous copy, the final copy is never the same as the original. The last copy would never be the same color as the original; in the same way, after all those years of living with that mentality, your fear, distrust, and envy should have faded, leaving only the positive. Therefore, there is no way we should still be suffering from slavery.

The lack of moral and ethical behavior and knowledge on the part of many Haitians is causing some of us to suffer more than others. In addition, they have never taken the time to reflect on and change their behaviors and attitudes like others have done around the world. Seriously, they should take a good deep breath, and think about changing the way they have been taught, not only at school, but especially at home. We should have overcome our slave mentality by now because it has been centuries since we were slaves. I guarantee that special change should bring more satisfaction in our environment.

In addition to that, our educational system needs more communication, respect, caring, sharing, and loving. School is not only about science, mathematics, and other subjects. In the same way that they are teaching those subjects, they could also be teaching cooperation by using collaborative learning activities, such as having the kids do their homework together as is usually the case in United States. This same technique of learning was utilized in Cuba, and the difference is discernable. Haitians need to learn to work together from daycare to university in order to remove the selfishness, the insecurity, and the anger so that they can say they are smarter than others. They need to stop criticizing and correcting, and start learning to help others. These types of anger are the main reasons that we have been so fully saturated with more crime and violence than any other place in the world. It is a guarantee that if we do not take our time to change the system and the way our educational system works we will remain the same that we are today in future generations.

Thus, how can we be expected to become a democratic country when democracy involves a basic respect of human rights? It seems we are expecting respect without teaching respect. It is the same as for our brothers who are spending their time in the military in Haiti; they all learn how to destroy and kill others by way of displaying power. They all have goals of using their power to steal and exploit others. With all of this, we can reach an understanding of those kinds of people who are worse than the slaves. None of the military constitute a better institution than the civilian slaves and the criminals. All of them have the same mentality and they will not go anywhere with those kinds of attitudes.

Furthermore, Haitian rulers would like to implant democracy in their country; the United States has been trying to help by maintaining a presence there, not only to stop Haitians from killing each other, but to help them keep the country in peace. The United States has so much courage and patience to be there to help, but that is not appreciated by any of the native military. One of the most prevalent qualities of illiteracy is the inability to appreciate what they have. Even most animals have the common sense to know how to appreciate their environment without being educated about the practice.-Do you think that, given everything I've just said, that we are ready for democracy? Are we ready for democracy when we don't even know the meaning and the sense of the word *appreciation*? I would like to see how it could happen without the nation being well-prepared.

When I say "being well-prepared," I mean aspects like a definite reform in education, where the government would take measures to institute such practices as placing a psychologist's and psychiatrist's office in each school district to evaluate the students. These professionals can refer the ones who have been determined to be psychosocially ill to psychiatric physicians for treatment before they become violent criminals. A psychiatric unit in each hospital is also needed, with qualified psychiatric medical doctors available. A good lab is also necessary, with several phlebotomists in each area clinic or hospital.

By accomplishing the above goals, the Haitian people might start down the road toward democracy because in order to have democracy in any country, every citizen would need to respect the rights of his or her fellow citizens as well as their dignity as human beings. When the people express their opinions, they should also listen to the views of other people, even people they might disagree with. Democracy requires a lot of compromises. Haitians must be able to sit down with one another and learn to negotiate. If they think that they can establish any form of democracy without all of that, they are fools. The peace corps is trying to help Haiti by working toward peace there before Haitians transform their own birthplace into a desert land. Generally speaking, no one has any intention of setting up a democracy in a place where the percentage of illiterate people has been 95 percent since before I was born. Just give me a break!

In addition to that, reformers would have to challenge the ideas of all the quacks over there who in the past had abused military service in Haiti. This is very helpful toward enacting democracy because getting rid of the abusers eliminates the power of the slave commander. The destruction of the army in Haiti reduced the overload of sexual predators in the country because those predators were the worst ones compared to other sexual predators around the world, believe it or not. They had so much power in everything, that they used to enter any family's home and have sex not only with the mother and the daughter, but also with the father, cousins, aunts, and grandmothers. If soldiers can imitate the slaves in any other country, wearing earrings, having dreadlocks, imitating rastafarian dance and music, I am sure that they are smart to imitate well the good way of living by stopping the violence and crime in our country. Haiti should be a model, since it was the first country to get independence. This message is only for the area of the world that contains the worst slavery history. Don't you think Cuba, which is about fifty kilometers from Haiti, is ready for democracy, because it has reached all the conditions and the requirements to do so? However, the Cuban government is still undecided about that; we all can understand why. As then Senator Obama always said in his presidential agenda, "It is just a word." Honestly, democracy is just a word for Cuba. In a country where this word has really taken birth, we might need to look carefully and be good listeners to be able to see there is nothing like democracy. In the U.S. Pledge of Allegiance, there is a phrase that says: "and to the republic for which it stands." There is no place where it says: "to the democracy for which it stands." Also, in *The Constitution*, the United States shall "guarantee to every state in this union a *republican* form of government (Article IV).

If we have common sense, my brothers and sisters, as the descendants of slaves, we all would change without need of the word "democracy." Again, Obama, in his presidential campaign, always used an important word: "change." This word is not only appropriate for America, but it also can be used in Haiti to indicate a change in our country, which means we will borrow it for the moment. For example, we have a system of abuse where, at school, all the professors use beating for discipline. Based upon experience, everyone that is abused may have, down the road, a tendency to abuse another. In fact, researchers and psychologists have proven the effects of abuse on those who were abused in the past. According to Graham-Bermann, an American psychologist specializing in post-traumatic stress in children exposed to family violence and single-event trauma: "Most of the children that were beaten in the past will develop post-traumatic stress disorder." In addition to that, "they will develop anxiety, sleep disorders, eating disturbances, nightmares, and so forth. Victims within this age group may also show a loss of interest in social activities, low self-esteem, withdrawal or avoidance of peer relations, rebelliousness, and oppositional-defiant behavior" (Graham-Bermann and Levendosky, 1998). Abuse also causes temper tantrums and irritability.

According to the researchers, those punishments will make children clingy and vulnerable to stress and exhibit abnormal function in the serotonin and norepinephrine system in the brain. In humans, these neurotransmitters are critical for the control of mood stability as well as anxiety and depression. I have no hesitation in joining the opposition to such practices, which are correctly condemned and labeled as child abuse. Most Haitians were abused and are aware of it, and this is the main reason that their behaviors become unacceptable in this society. Without a reform in both education and health care, it will be impossible for Haiti to become a democratic country. They really are not aware of it. They are so innocent that they have no clue what causes them to act so badly. Today, they are becoming the worst criminals and the worst slaves. I ask for a pardon for the nation; please give Haiti a chance, the country that was placed next to heaven, but today is actually one exit before hell.

Food Supply

Haiti is a tropical country that can produce anything that it wants. What is the main reason today that all of its citizens are crying for foods? They all depend on exported foods. Where are their natural foods? The people of Haiti can be doctors, engineers, or whatever and still have the ability to plant and keep animals. But as professionals, they will encourage the nonprofessionals to plant because they know how to do it better.

The U.S. government and UN World Food Program promised a combined total of $117 million this year in food and agricultural aid that included more than 40,000 tons of beans, rice, and other food intended to quell the emergency. Paul Farmer said that, "Haiti, once the world's largest exporter of sugar and other tropical produce to Europe, began importing even sugar from U.S. controlled sugar production in the Dominican Republic and Florida. It was terrible to see Haitian farmers put out of work" (Bill Quigley, 2008).

"We are providing Haiti with a shipment of food in the next hours," announced the president of the Bolivarian Republic of Venezuela, Hugo Chavez, on April 12, during the Meeting of Intellectuals and Artists for the Latin American Peace and Sovereignty, held in Caracas. "Haiti, the first Latin American and Caribbean Republic (it achieved its independence from France in February, 1804), is Latin America's and the Caribbean's poorest nation, with an average per capita income below US$2" Mark Schuller 2008) (Schuller 2008). Shame! Shame! I would like that the slave descendants try the best they can to change their mentality in order to save the future generation and to bring more success to their environment. By not doing so it might encourage me to write a second book. However, I don't believe that we would like me to put our additional secrets out since I am fully loaded with what I have seen and witnessed over there. Besides, we certainly know that all of them are wrong, and people must know about it for the safety of everyone on this planet. Today, I find opportunity to write a small amount of it: down the road if there is no change on our behavior, the quantity of secrets that I will write about our country will be ten times this book. This is telling you if I put some of them out, we might seriously lose the nation, and you would never find a way to obtain it back because we are very dangerous. I ask a pardon for the nation, but do not give me an opportunity to condemn the nation for wrongdoing because you might find a hard time living anywhere in this planet. The very first thing is to cultivate the trust between other nations. Every human being must trust someone in the essence of life since animals are trusted by us and themselves. Being true to ourselves becomes naturally a form of trust and belief that can lead us to freedom eternally.

One of the important verbal abuses they have not been able to stop is when they accuse someone of killing the dead. They are unable to recognize that we all have to go when our time is expired. They are still in a country of all abuses.

Haiti used to be named "paradise des Antilles," where tourists from all over the world used to come and spend time at the hotel and the Club Mediterranean. Today, we can simply call it a country of all abuses, diseases, and crimes. There are all kinds of abuse on the island. That is unbelievable! In another way, they have been corrupted by being the "abuse creator" and "crime inventor." They think that they all are here on this earth permanently, but when we are born on this earth, we don't realize that we have come with a complete roundtrip ticket to assure our return.

Another common abuse in the region is sexual abuse, which is considered the main form of abuse. For example, Haitian men have babies in every corner of the streets just to show that they are "*macho men*." Rape is also a part of their nature. They used to call it *Kadejak*, which meant "to scarify a woman sexually," at the time that I was living there. The way that they used to operate was that they usually met together at one place where they were all known and a girl might be there. There probably would be at least fifteen of them that would pass the girl from one to the other, while one of them held her down. It was estimated that eighty percent of the women had been raped during the time that I was living on the island. According to Lizette Robleto, Progressio's Latin America and Caribbean advocacy coordinator, "The Haitian government is failing to take HIV and AIDS seriously and urgently needs to tackle the increase in sexual assaults and rape which puts women at risk of infection (Robleto, 2008). I was one of the few who was not a victim because the rapists were afraid of my parents.

Most of the men are sexual predators because all of them believe in the superiority of virgin girls. They all want fourteen-year-old girls because the men have to be able to feel and visualize the hymen in the vagina. In addition, there are a few Haitian men who live outside of Haiti and travel with enough money each year just for the search of virgin girls.

There are a few who are licensed medical doctors in the United States who were born in the same town where I was born that had sex with and took the virginity of twenty-three little girls. Those men were at least sixty-four years old, and those little girls were between nine and twelve years old. Those doctors had paid each of them twenty dollars to have sex with them so they could remove the hymen. Most of the Haitians have pleasure on removing hymen, and most of them are uncomfortable when they are seen with kids. In general, the country of Haiti definitely needs a reform in its administration for these abusers by putting rules, regulations, fines, and strong sanctions on the violators without prejudice. When I say without prejudice, I mean: "no money under the table or behind closed doors."

Voodoo Practice

I would never disagree with the practice of voodoo in Haiti because everyone has his or her own beliefs that should be understood. Voodoo plays an important role in a community where they have no other entertainment better than that. Also, they have no electricity where they can watch what is going on around the world and learn new things. Therefore, it is considered a form of unity where everyone can understand the needs of the others in the region. They all meet together at one place, have fun together, talk to each other, and learn new things from each other. It is like a sharing meeting in the other sense where all of them can dance together. Again, they can share ideas and inform the others about what is happening on the other side of town, since the country is so small and transportation is virtually nonexistent.

However this practice, at the same time, contains more abuse and exploitation than you can ever imagine. Psychologically, it is the worst abuse because they pretend that they are possessed of the voodoo spirits in order to convince the people. Would you believe there is a federal case of voodoo spirits in a country that has justice? First of all, they know that there is nothing like that: they are tricking another fool who is worse than them. Also, most of the voodoo priests travel to Haiti just to go to buy "dead body." They pass it at the airport in the form of powder because they burn the entire body: it mixes with several snakes, cockroaches, frogs, and lizards. This powder passes at the airport in the form of coffee in a coffee container. They sell one teaspoon for one thousand dollars; this particular powder is very useful and very dangerous in their community, and its function is to destroy human beings. They call it *"kout poudre"* which means *"powder sender.*" They might give it to you if you are cheating with their husband. They might give it to you if they have any type of problem with you. For by example, they give their cars to the body shop to fix and the mechanic didn't do a good job; They charge them too much or the job wasn't done properly. They might get a *"kout poudre."I surprise United States government didn't put any restriction on voodoo organization*

*in this country because the crime investigators should inspect them very often.
Those* types of exploitation are punishable and intolerable in any country that is committed to the protection of its citizens. Second, if they really felt that they had those voodoo spirits in their mind or that they had talked to them in a dream or whatever, they might be suffering from some type of either schizophrenia or delusion because it is impossible to see something that doesn't even exist. Also, most voodoo practitioners are alcoholics, and the alcohol that they are imbibing is mixed with several potent leaves and many other alcohols. This combination would probably make them see anything because it is a potentially dangerous combination. In *Science Daily* (November 14, 2001), David Pearson, a researcher in the Human Performance Laboratory, wrote: "Mixing powerful stimulants contained in some energy drinks with depressants in alcohol could cause cardiopulmonary or cardiovascular failures."

Those who pretend these spirits exist would be the last to know because they do not have enough electricity to use television in the country. However, the astronauts that travel to the other planets would probably meet those spirits before them. If devil spirits really existed, one day you would see that they would come with several proofs to show and announce it on the TV news, and then everyone might know about it. At this point, anyone could broadcast that they have communicated with the spirits; they would find the entire world following them wondering what it is about. Right now, because there is no proof, it is considered a fake ceremony. Between me and you, we can simply define the word *voodoo* as a way of survival for the nonprofessional slaves that live in the jungle. Voodoo practitioners can also be intellectuals who are dedicated to steal, live by trickery, and exploit innocents. You might call those special intellectuals *chupacabra,* a Puerto Rican word meaning "goat suckers." In this case, we will use it here for the tricksters and exploiters and give it a new definition: *human suckers.*

Moreover, voodoo adherents complain that they had been oppressed by slavery, which is the reason all of us have suffered from fear, distrust, and envy. That statement is not true and hard to believe because when the slaves entered Haiti, they moved in with a part of the voodoo belief. The new generation then became more knowledgeable about it. This practice is so powerful today that they have found a way to transform human beings into zombies. In addition, most of the men in Haiti live with fear, distrust, and envy because they are always thinking someone can kill them. They use the superpower of the devil in order to get stronger so that they can stop anyone who otherwise might kill them.

Voodoo Organization

The *sanprel* in Haiti comprises kids, adults, and old people, forming a gang every Wednesday and Friday night to obtain more instructions from their voodoo priest. Those meetings are held at midnight in two sections of each town. They usually take place in order to train the participants until they reach the stage where they can disappear if they are engaged in any situation where the ancient devils are trying to get rid of them by trying to eat one of them. The voodoo priest composes something with the blood of the dead and passes it around to them one by one to drink. At the same time, the meeting is a class to teach them prayers that they might need to know and passwords if they need them to meet the higher levels of the other voodoo societies because voodoo has many other societies and classes in it.

One of the groups is called *Zobop;* this group is a dangerous group. If others do not know their passwords when they meet a member of *Zobop*, they may face death because *Zobops* are there just to look for one of them to eat. Another group *is 3 jambes;* this group is a higher class than the *Zobops*. Higher still are the *galiportes* (lit., "giant dogs"), who are humans that transform into giant dogs so they eat small dogs. On the *National Geographic* channel, you see that the big animals eat the medium ones, and the medium one eats the smaller ones, which is part of survival skills. They adopted the same technique in voodoo, not only to eat people, but to use young boys for homosexuality.

There is another group called *Roi Minuit;* they are the higher ones who are only out during the Christmas season looking for anyone from any of the groups to eat. There is also the *vlingbindin* group. This group meets one day per year, and regardless of how far apart they live, they still have to meet together to receive their secret mystic degrees. All of them are classified as cannibals, and most of them are bisexual, homosexual, and lesbians. With all of these practices and beliefs, do people still believe that the fear, distrust, and envy came from slavery? Who might be able to end these types of violence and crime in Haiti?

The answer is very simple: our honorable brother Fidel Castro. In the same way he stopped gambling, homosexuality, alcohol, and prostitution in his country, he probably would use the same techniques to end the crimes in Haiti, which are worse than the ones he destroyed in his country. I would like to know if scientists with the new technologies can possibly find a way to clone him and place a new Castro in Haiti to reform the nation in order to have peace on the island. I would choose him because he is the only leader so far who has strong views on morality, has a strong heart, and has the patience to discipline anyone who cannot behave nicely in society. In Cuba they also practice voodoo, but in the same way that the Africans slaves introduced it. They use it for dance, folklore, and so on, but no one takes advantage of it by killing someone because their leader would probably hang them before they could even think about something like that. In fact, they also practice it in the United States, but they have not taken a chance so far to sacrifice anyone.

The nation is powerfully entrenched in voodoo, but they have been illiterate since their independence in 1804. They have been unable to come with something new and positive, with such power that all of them can share as a heritage. Many countries in the world have had advances in technology, astronomy, and so forth. How did they come so far after crime and violence? A demon mind quality fully includes selfishness, lust, anger, greed, pride, jealousy, fear, slander, base thoughts, aggressiveness, cruelty, cheating, lying, hypocrisy, animosity, enviousness, division, and so forth. All of those are fully classified as diseases. By connecting to all of those issues, they have totally lost their moral values, and they will definitely lose the nation one day.

It is a psychological ego that would pass from generation to generation. If they could give up this power crop, they probably would be able to live pleasant lives where they can really enjoy life in this beautiful earth that God has created. The entire country is doing the opposite of God's command, which results in leading the nation into poverty, drugs, alcohol, prostitution, violence, crime, sin, and loss of spirituality.

Restoration of the Democracy

Let us pretend that we would like to restore democracy in Haiti and organize an adequate administration where everyone will be treated with respect and dignity. In order to do so, what ingredients would be needed? It would not be as easy a job as everyone might think. A lot of patience, money, solidarity, and so on will be needed. In spite of that, this is our country, and it should be our job, poor or rich. We all should unify together and move on toward the country's needs. People do not have any obligation to take my advice, but I would still send the message because I feel I should do so. Another thing, it might be difficult to stop violence in Haiti; however, there is a way to stop it and have the democracy restored at the same time. Here are a few simple plans that might need to be considered in order to start.

A serious administration with competent employees would be needed, which means all the employees must have a clean background check, good character and morals, and a blood check. Each should be evaluated by a psychiatrist before hiring in order to avoid future violent cases. Generally speaking, in the past, there was not enough thought given to forming a formal administration, since the new leaders always applied the same old techniques from the time of their independence. In fact, their old technique was to take anyone that had paid them for any employment without having that person properly trained for a particular position.

A Department of Social Services in each district and town is needed to control the security of the children and the families in the region. This department should have a police station and a federal office to investigate any crimes that might occur in the environment. They might need to ask every citizen in that region to come to fill out a form that will contain all their information including their fingerprints, date of birth, references, addresses, and family members. That information should be placed on file after being documented and computerized. Continuing to have unknown citizens in the country is a dangerous situation in which authorities would never be aware of who had committed any type of crime, and no sanction would ever be applied because they would be unable to identify or locate the perpetrators. Finally, I would recommend them to establish the death penalty in Haiti since they have been overloaded with criminals. According to Frantz Robert Monde, a congressman from Nippes, when asked what he thought the government could do to respond to the population's concerns, said: "I and other congressman are presenting legislation to Congress to call on the president to exercise extra-constitutional powers and introduce the death penalty for kidnapping. This is not permitted under our Constitution. It is not historically in our nature. Yet this is an extraordinary crime wave and we wish to have it stop" (Roebling, 2008).

The regulations on visitors that travel in the country need to be changed. People who enter the country should be known and identified to avoid suspected violence. They should fill out an application upon their entrance that has a complete address and the family members, friends, or organizations with whom they are going to stay or work. If they are going to spend more than a week, a copy of their passport should be documented and placed on file for further investigation. We should develop forensic labs to learn techniques of how to study a crime scene, because it is not advisable to accuse anyone who might be innocent.

The school system should be changed by eliminating things that they do not need, such as having students memorize everything. Rather, they need to do projects on the history of Haiti. Students can learn much more by doing projects instead of memorizing chapter per chapter. By using the project technique, the students would be able to improve their understanding and heighten their ability to learn better. The length of high school and elementary school would be shortened, and there would be more students ready for university each year.

Psychologists, social workers, and nurses should be placed in each school district for the needs of the students. A first-aid kit should be available for the students. The teachers should attend continuing education seminars regularly in order to keep their jobs. Teachers in Haiti are not well trained. They become teachers without any formal school training. They just keep teaching the same thing every year until they memorize it. I remember that my mathematics professor in high school used to come without the book to teach the class. He had been a professor since 1935, teaching the same math over and over, but he had no clue how to demonstrate any of those formulas. He asked us to memorize everything, and he might call the students who were unable to memorize it *pipter* a word that means "little prostitute."

These students were fourteen to fifteen years old. It is a sad situation to be born in a place where they only have ignorant people teaching.

Family meetings should be maintained at all times and they should always be given a pamphlet that has all the rules and regulations of the country. What would happen in case any of the laws had been violated? We should make sure that everyone understands the rules and regulations of the country before punishing anyone.

Citizens need to stay up to date about those laws because the government might try to create another form of abuse with those rules and regulations and make the situation worse than it was without them. They need to put rules and regulations on everything in the country: for example, anyone that kills someone should have the death sentence as punishment. We have more criminals than anywhere in the world. If Haiti established and enforced the death sentence, they might not have any citizens remaining! There are also good people in Haiti, but they are probably only five to eight percent of the population. Haiti does not have any capability to develop good political candidates. They may have good skills and be well prepared professionally, but when it comes to character, morality, and ethics, most of them would be nullified. All of the current leaders have been corrupted, especially with the above types of abuse and voodoo problems. No one would be able to believe them even if they became a Protestant. They might change religion just to catch innocents. They are too smart about abuse, crime, and violence. We used to have a pastor who was having sex with a little girl in the church, and when she got pregnant, he forced someone in that church to marry the girl. We also had several sexual predator priests. Unfortunately, even pastors cannot escape the stigma that most Haitian males are sexual predators.

With regard to marriage, if you are not a virgin, Haitian men will not marry you. The virgins are only those females under eighteen, so this reinforces the fact that all of the men are sexual predators. I never got hurt, not only because my parents were very strong but also because I was very independent.

Anyone who fights for any reason should be arrested, pay fines, and be put in jail. They should be required to pay money for bail in order to reduce criminal activity, because we all know the secret that we do not like to pay for anything. They should have to spend ten years in jail without prejudice if they do not have any money available for bail. These prisoners should clean airports, streets, plant flowers, clean schools, hospitals, and so on.

While they are in prison, they should be checked by psychiatrists and be medicated if they pose a threat to themselves or others; otherwise, when they come out, they may have bigger problems.

Further, anyone who is involved in a rape or kidnapping should have shackles on their feet and hands for at least seven months after their arrest. They should stay in jail for thirty years or more. Before coming back to the public life, they should also be treated by a professional psychiatrist.

Any kind of abuse toward children should ultimately be penalized by a death sentence. Sexual abuse to children should be punished by more than fifty years of incarceration followed by a death sentence. Prisoners might be released if their behavior changed while they were in jail. They would need to be able to function as human beings in society before they could be released. They would have to show improvement in cooperation, feeling, attentiveness, and so forth. They would also need to have daily activities created for them to be productively employed.

The government might need to create factories in jails in which prisoners could work and produce something that might be beneficial for the citizens of the country, such as clothing. In addition, any citizen who is in jail for any reason would not be able to leave the country upon release, because they might continue the same behavior in another country. As soon as criminals are arrested, they should have their pictures and their fingerprints taken for identification in case they become flight risks. Runaway prisoners would also need to be punished by a death sentence.

Finally, any citizens of the nation who sacrifice their own newborn kids in the Mayan tradition should be immediately executed; the Mayan civilization existed three thousand years ago when no laws against the practice existed. However, the Maya did not only sacrifice human beings: they also made calendars and left some very useful information for the future generations. Also, some of them were astrologists who left information that NASA uses today. In fact, although they did not know to read and write, their culture and advancements make this generation interested in reading their history.

In contrast, with the voodoo practice that has been adopted for several years in Haiti, nothing has been accomplished so far except the violence, murder, sex, orgies, and crimes. At this moment in time, everyone in the world should be aware that such crimes as the sacrifice of a child are classified as murders where the perpetrators should be condemned and face a death sentence. We all know that at the Haitian white house every year, these sacrifices take place, and in fact, thousands of children have lost their lives. In the *Canada Free Press* (June 28, 2005), editor Judy McLeod said that ex-president Aristide professed in a speech to Congress attendees: "Voodoo is one of the great religions in the world alongside Christianity, Islam, and Judaism, and also announced funding for a national voodoo temple." It should be noted that Aristide, "a defrocked priest earlier in 1995 had renounced the Catholic Church and said he was returning to the voodoo faith of his ancestors." In July of the same year, he held a large voodoo congress at the National Palace attended by over 300 leading *houngans* and *bocors* (black magicians—including leaders of the dreaded Bizango Cult, which practices zombification and human sacrifice). Both Aristide's renunciation of the Catholic Church and his voodoo congress, while widely publicized in the Haitian press, were completely suppressed in the American news media. One account that circulated in Port-au-Prince is that when Aristide dedicated the "secret well" before Clinton's visit he "shed the blood of a newborn infant in gratitude to the gods whom he believes allowed his return to power." This report is widely accepted by the Haitian people as fact according to Joel A. Ruth (1998). He also mentioned that "it is a religion based on prayer, music, dancing, and sacrifices, often bloody, and that it is an essential part of national identity." Finally, he mentioned that voodoo "was the root of their independence" (Lowell Ponte, 2004). (Ponte 2004)

A decree was issued in 1935 to stop this practice. When President Duvalier was elected, he actually was one of the voodoo believers who had really returned to it during 1957, but he had used it in a different way in order to have and to hold the power for life by having all the voodoo priests and their participants become free secret service agents. Since he knew that eighty-five percent of the population was practicing this nonsense, he used most of those illiterates to spy for him. He also sacrificed many kids, because he made himself a voodoo priest. According to Richard Bovet, in *Carnival of Terrors (p. 127)*, he was rumored to drink human blood and devour human flesh in the privacy of his own quarters.

Mental Illnesses and Drug Effects

Geographically speaking, Haiti is close to Colombia, which supplies the bulk of drugs, including cocaine, heroin, marijuana, and others. In fact, Haiti is becoming the main sector for the transfer of narcotics to other countries. Many of those substances cause damage to the brain cells. As all of us know, the drugs cannot be bought or sold without being tested, which proves that Colombia is actually overloaded with narcotics and becoming the richest country from distributing them.

According to a study published in 2005, "the small arms survey estimated that as many as 170,000 small arms are held illegally in Haiti. Haitians have so many drugs that they can trade them for guns with Jamaica" Davis (2008)

According to Sandra Blakeslee (2007), "The 'insular cortex' is the smallest part of the brain, the same size as the Haitian fifty-cent piece, and is responsible for interpretation of body sensation and other stimuli. In addition to that, a part of the frontal lobe is also responsible for giving us a sense of homeostatic functions, and the anterior insular cortex contains a population of neurons."

Dealers might need to understand the important part of the brain that is destroyed by inhaling narcotic drugs before buying and selling them. The effects of inhalants will eventually paralyze the individual's ability to learn, remember, and solve problems. Many of these drugs cause euphoria, tremors, panic, and disorientation. According to John A. Harvey and Barry E. Kosofsky (1998), these drugs can also lead to feelings of paranoia and anxiety and reduce the ability to feel pleasure which most users probably already have, given the way they are acting in society. Although often used to enhance sex drive, physical effect of cocaine on the receptors in the brain reduces the ability to feel pleasure, which in turn causes the dependency on the drug.

Usage of Antibiotics

Most of the Haitians like to use antibiotics, and these particular medications are only available by prescription. However, everyone must still have a complete lab workup in order to know which one would be good for the problem that they might have. This practice is controversial in Haiti, because if they (Haitians) might have a cold or sore throat, they are buying antibiotics for it. According to scientists and biologists, however, Antibiotics only work against infections caused by bacteria, fungus and by certain parasites. They don't work against any infections caused by viruses. Viruses cause colds, the flu and most coughs and sore throats. (Hooten and Levy, 2001). Because colds are caused by viruses, antibiotics are ineffective. Antibiotics are powerful medicines used to treat some infections. However, antibiotics can be harmful when they are not used the right way. In fact, "antibiotics themselves can also cause some germ-related problems, such as yeast infections of the vagina and mouth, and a severe form of diarrhea. Antibiotics should only be used when prescribed by a health care provider to treat bacterial infections," according to the Cleveland Clinic Foundation (2009).

The important part of this case is that antibiotics can probably cause allergic reactions that may be fatal. In fact, the severity of antibiotics' side effects is not only rashes, but also anaphylaxis, a life threatening condition in which it becomes difficult to breathe. The more serious of the side effects is the formation of kidney stones with sulphonomides, abnormal blood clotting with some of the cephalosporins, increasing sensitivity to the sun with tetracyclines, blood disorders with trimetropin, and deafness with erythromycin and aminoglycosides. As Dr. John I. Pitt (1979), said, "Antibiotics kill your body's good bacteria too, leading to serious health risks," which tells us that each time that we use an antibiotic, the immune system would definitely become further suppressed, because antibiotic kills our good microflora bacteria in our body, not only the pathogenic bacteria. With the absence of the microflora, you might be targeted by any other infections, because its job is to strengthen the immune system and keep the pathogenic disease of the intestinal track in good health. According to an official from the National Institutes of Health and the Centers for Disease Control, "the ratio of protective bacteria to harmful bacteria should be high, at least 80% protective bacteria to 20% harmful bacteria (Wassenaar, 2002). Unfortunately, in many people, this ratio is reversed, with the result that harmful chemicals are constantly entering the bloodstream and toxifying the body. Based on the information by Wassenaar 2009, "After the use of it the body will have no more than 20% friendly and 80% bad one if not more." Most illnesses, diseases, and problems begin in the intestinal tract, thus, antibiotics create the opportunity for serious illness to intervene.

It is very important to know that many patients who have psychiatric disorders used to be treated by infectious disease physicians. Janet Ginsburg on *Newsweek International* (December 1, 2005) pronounced that bacteria, viruses, and parasites may cause mental illness, such as depression, autism, and anorexia. They have evidence that infections might play more of an integral role in mental illness than they thought in the past. "Scientists have long known that some diseases can cause behavioral problems. When penicillin was first used to treat syphilis, thousands of cured schizophrenics were released from mental asylums. Now, however, scientists have evidence that infections may play a far bigger role in mental illness than previously thought. They've linked cases of obsessive-compulsive disorder, bipolar disorder, and schizophrenia to a variety of infectious agents, and they're investigating autism, Tourette's, and anorexia as well" (,Janet Ginsburg, 2005) (Ginsburg 2005). According to a new study by Steve Mitchell (2008), MSNBC contributor, "a blood test could be used to diagnose and assess the severity of certain mental illnesses, such as bipolar disorder. Either way, if anyone has serious mental disorders that are untreated, they might become a danger to themselves and others."

In general, people with psychotic disorders might have an imbalance of certain chemicals in the brain. According to scientists, they may be either very sensitive to or produce too much of a chemical called dopamine. In fact, dopamine is a neurotransmitter, a substance that really helps the nerve cells in the brain: its main function is to send messages to each other. An imbalance of dopamine would definitely affect the the way brain reacts to certain stimuli, such as sounds, smells, and sights. In general, Haiti is in great need of a psychiatric hospital, because most of the Haitians are acting in an abnormal way. Most of them are already becoming out of control, and one day in the future, we might face a situation where no one would be able to save any of the Haitians.

As a result of the above data, the United Nations is wasting money that they could probably invest in other necessities, and on top of that, the United States government is losing some good elements that are working for peacekeeping forces. If the Haitians were smart, they would promise peace and ask the United Nations to give them a hand in developing the country. However, they all lack knowledge and financial skills, so they would never be able to reach any form of development in the country.

Everyone can verify that the slave mentality that came from Africa over five centuries ago still exists in Haiti from generation to generation, because Haitians are unable to make a change to the system, and they are proud to be that way. If we look around the world, we can see that all African immigrants have not changed, including some of them who are living in United States; they have the same mentality and eat the same foods without having a plan to change.

One notable exception is in Cuba, where the slave descendants look different and think differently. All the slaves in Cuba were born with a strong and a durable mind: they all needed a mind that was stronger than theirs that they could easily follow, which made President Castro a "slave reformer." He is the only one they would obey in the world, because he is tough on his decision. The United States made laws that protect everyone, even the criminals, when they tried their best to satisfy anyone. With Haiti's laws, criminals have a free ride to commit more crimes. Some prisons in America are like hotels, where the U.S. government makes sure everyone has been fed. If a prisoner is an immigrant, after serving his term, he would be deported, in which case he would have a free ride to go back home.

Birth Records

Logically, every country should have birth and death records available. Since independence, Haiti has had only one birth records office in the country, which has no value for anybody because there is no Haitian that truly has a complete birth certificate. This is the reason most Haitians change their birthplace anytime they want for any reason. Most of the times they choose to do it because they want to show they were born in a city, not in a rural section. Sometimes they are listed in the crime list, but they need to travel to other countries, in which case they would change their birth place before they would even think about leaving the country. By not having a section for vital records, the government would not be able to locate any citizen in the country.

Birth records play an important role in any administration, because they provide and ensure accountability to the public and promote public participation in public health activities and decision-making. In addition to that, they would be able to locate anyone who committed any type of crime. If they had paid anyone to make a birth certificate, they would have it ready, and they could change the date and the birthplace, which makes no sense in a country that has been independent for several years.

How can Haitians be ready for democracy when they are unable to locate any citizen in the country? How would they be able to provide safety for other citizens and visitors? Visitors play an integral role for a country; they not only bring business, but they also like to invest and spend when they're visiting. Tourism has many advantages by providing employment for citizens in bars, hotels, as well as working as tour guides. This would also change the standard of living for people by growing their economy and further lowering the dependency ratio.

If a country has high employment, it might be able to focus on other objectives like education, healthcare, roads, and other concerns. They would also provide indirect employment in terms of factory workers in order to produce goods and services in the economy. With that, they would increase demands of the population and the tourists. Again, tourists like to have souvenirs that are handmade and that can be produced by citizens. The farmers would also encourage growing more foods for the population and the visitors as well. Much needed foreign currency and foreign investment would be increased, which would also benefit the economy. As a result of that, they would need to have access to birth records in every hospital where the births had occurred. Haitians should take advantage of technology by having birth records registered, not only in writing, but in an electronic database in alphabetic order, region by region, town by town, and city by city.

The Desire for Freedom

Everybody is crying for freedom around the world. We all live in a world where everyone must obey all the laws, which makes it very easy to understand. Even the spirits, if they really existed, would need to obey the laws of their spirit commander. Also the dead must live under their own laws, rules, and regulations if there is really life after death. The military has to accept the orders of their generals and their government as well. Further, women must obey their husbands according to the Bible. In general, regardless whether you are situated in heaven or hell, everyone must follow specific guidelines.

Freedom does not mean just being able to do anything you want. "For Sartre, because we are free in every situation, we are also responsible for our own 'essence' or the choices that we make. However, the weight of our own freedom, or the 'nothingness of being,' can also lead to 'bad faith.'" In other words, we all are free (R. Pitt, 2005).

You Haitians are attempting to deceive yourselves and act as if you aren't free. During slavery, all of the slaves thought that they were not free; in reality, they were free because they had made their own choices to become slaves. They called it "slavery" because they did not receive any salary. In fact, since they did not have any skills at that time, they did not deserve any monetary compensation.

On the other hand, it was also an opportunity to learn about different parts of the world and develop skills for future generations. Realistically, they had given birth to values by revolting against them. In most traditional approaches, they had made a work of art out of obtaining their independence. In fact, they like slavery so much that they are still traveling to the Dominican Republic to continue to work as slaves. One million Haitians are working in the Dominican Republic sugar plantations.

According to a study published by the UNICEF National Planning Office in 1999, "50,000 Haitian girls aged twelve to sixteen were sold for prostitution and slavery to the Dominican Republic. Most of them worked as cane cutters, domestics, shoe shiners, and so on" (U.S. Department of State, 2004). In the past, they worked for several years as slaves in Cuba.

Today they are complaining that they all suffered from slavery, which is wrong, because it seems that they all liked being slaves. Indeed, there might be more slaves around than ever before. "Benjamin Skinner (2008) has said that, 'In 1850, a slave would cost roughly $30,000 to $40,000. Today you can go to Haiti and buy a nine-year-old girl to use as a sexual and domestic slave for $50. The devaluation of human life is incredibly pronounced"

Most of us believe that slavery no longer exists, but it is still alive, believe it or not. According to the London-based Anti-Slavery International (ASI) (,Charles Jacobs 2006) (Jacobs 2006) the world's oldest human-rights organization, "there are at least twenty-seven million people in bondage. In fact, from Khartoum to Calcutta, and from Brazil to Bangladesh, men, women, and children are living and working as slaves."

In spite of that, everyone around the world has in their mind that Cuban Communism is not free. They all are wrong; because Cubans can go anywhere they want safely. President Castro is not only a leader for his country, but also an honorable father for the Cuban nation by providing safety for its citizens even when they leave. He makes sure that they are well-educated and well-prepared before they leave their country, which is fair enough. His plan was not to have Cuban citizens pick tomatoes and become cane cutters in other countries. His great idea was to keep the nation together and make it a model for other nations. In fact, he achieved his goal by having a better health care plan than any other nation, according to the World Health Organization (2000). The World Health Organization had also mentioned that "Cuba provides a doctor for every 170 residents, and has the second highest doctor to patient ratio in the world after Italy" (BBC News January 17, 2006). In fact, "in 1980, Cuban scientists had discovered a vaccine against meningitis B; the U.S. Treasury Department licensed the vaccine in 1999. The pharmaceutical company Smith-Kline Beecham made a deal in order to develop the vaccine for use in the United States and other countries."

From the day of independence to now, Haiti has had several leaders whom we all know. None of them ever thought about education and health care for their citizens. Today all Haitian citizens are crying for democracy. How can they choose their own president while they all have poor judgment?

They are unruly and unstable. They sell drugs and refuse to be educated. This is not a foundation for good democracy.

Aggressive Behavior

Aggressive behavior is an integral issue for the nation. In fact, it started with our parents and the way they all disciplined their children. Another important factor is that most Haitian men father their kids and then abandon them at birth. According to study coauthor Jon Hussey (2008), research assistant professor of maternal and child health in the UNC School of Public Health and a fellow at the Carolina Population Center, "Aggression—arguing, cruelty to others, destruction of property, disobedience, threatening people, and fighting or physically attacking others—was based on perceptions of the child's primary caregiver, who was interviewed when the child was aged 4, 6, and 8." In Haiti, another reason why most act in a violent manner is because of the way they are taught either at school or at home, and most were abandoned in childhood. Honestly, the nation has several problems.

Like Candidate Obama always said, "a change needs to take place." I would especially borrow this word "change" and use it for Haiti, because the situation will be worse in the future without it. If you really pay attention, you would be able to see that most Haitian men have a tendency to have a constantly negative attitude toward everything. They are always blaming others for their problems. They always have the feeling that others are making unreasonable demands on them, but they think they are the only ones who are doing a better job than what they are given credit for.

More than half of the country lacks self-confidence, and they live in fear. Aggression is a complex social behavior, and it can also signal other clinically defined conditions, such as bipolar disorder or post-traumatic stress disorder. As we all can imagine at this point, those particular problems did not come from slavery, but by the way all the oppressors had been taught.

Prejudice

Haiti is the same size as Maryland, is smaller than Cuba, and has half of Cuba's population. A small portion of the population has been divided into several groups with a lot of prejudices. In fact, Haiti has all kind of prejudices, and this is the main reason the intellectuals and the professionals have left the country after their graduation from the university. First of all, Haiti has three classes: lower class, middle class, and high class (bourgeoisie). Second, Haiti has two main Christian religious groups: Catholic (bourgeoisie) and Protestant (middle class mixed with low class); they are mixed with lower class because Protestants or Baptists are formed with the group of people that lost their Catholic status for bad behavior, like having a boyfriend, cheating, adultery, or because one of the family members becoming pregnant without being married. The priest would automatically discontinue communion for any of those complaints.

Catholicism is a religion for a loyal class that does not tolerate any bad behavior. Anyone would need to be very loyal and classy in order to survive as a Catholic Church member. Therefore, Catholics do not deal with Protestants. Jehovah's Witnesses do not have any class in Haiti; they can only deal with their own kind of Jehovah. We have Adventists that cannot marry with outsiders; they also deal with their own kind. The Episcopal Church also deals with its own. The voodooist is the only one in Haiti who can get anyone regardless of whether you are rich, Protestant, Catholic, middle class, or poor, because as long as you can contact them, you can also sleep in the same bed with them. Business people also only deal with their own group. In addition, intellectuals, who represent a small percentage of the population, find it hard to fit in; they need to run away before the illiterates (ninety-five percent of the population) cook all of them. The quantity of the lower class is too large, and that is where the violence and crime are occurring; no one would have a chance to survive if they were trying to get you, because most of them are mentally ill and not even aware of that. Also any politician or leader would be on their side because they are numerous, and they can vote and push any candidates.

In addition to that, intellectuals usually will not deal with uneducated people, which make the situation really tough. In Haiti, Catholics will not marry Baptists, and the lower class would never meet with the upper class. In general, we have too much prejudice in Haiti, and Haitians are always complaining about the United States with its prejudice, which is wrong, because it is only about race and color. We must honestly conclude that all of us on this earth will suffer prejudice on various levels.

When we do not know someone well, we unconsciously begin to characterize the person based on what we can see with our eyes; but since the world has become civilized with the emphasis on science and technology, we should wait until we truly know each individual before making any judgment. Knowledge about a person should make a difference in our opinion regardless of race, color, and nationality. In fact, discrimination is an illegal act in most western democracies, while discriminating between people on the basis of merit is lawful. For me, discrimination is a full stop sign in that if humans did not perpetuate discrimination, we would probably reach the end of the humanity by now. Imagine, for example, the number of diseases that exist on this earth and what would happen if all of us loved each other without prejudice. It would be catastrophic. Diseases would be able to multiply and even spread all over the earth and destroy all of us if we did not have some deterrent to unrestrained passion. As a result of that, anyone who has caught any type of infectious diseases either in Haiti or the United States has done so because he did not have any form of prejudice that prevented him from sleeping around with whoever was willing.

Creation of Values

Morality controls all acts, whether good or bad. It has been more than an era since Haiti has been living in a distressed situation where its people are fighting each other. In order to gain back the values they obtained by revolting against slavery, they would need to create again a system of values from which their kids and their grandkids would benefit. We all have learned the importance of morality, personality, and values and how important they are for a country.

We have come to a time where the slaves are totally out of control; without values, the country may face a terrible situation that no one would be able to overcome. In fact, Haitians have just started a new deal in the market where they sell their twelve- to sixteen-year-old girls in the Dominican Republic for prostitution. All of those kids will be destroyed with sexually transmitted diseases. Everyone is aware of what will happen in the future with someone who has been contaminated with a sexually transmitted disease. Most of the time those infections are so aggressive that they usually cause damage to the brain as well as the body.

Reforming morality in all of the slave neighborhoods would be a formal starting point in reeducating all the slaves who have been immoral and rebellious from generation to generation. At this point, leaving all of them the same way would damage the society and be a strong deterrent to peace. But our primary obligation should be to delegate forces to keep peace. It would be an act of compassion and kindness to rehabilitate them by placing some mental services at their convenience so all of them can finally find treatment.

Violence is the exertion of physical force that includes abuse and crime. It is abnormal for anyone to commit a crime, which is easy enough for anyone to understand. Scientists, biologists, and others have not only condemned violence as a form of insanity but they have also studied the causes of violence and what precautions should be taken in order to prevent it. By law, it is unacceptable for anyone to commit a crime, and criminals should be punished.

Slave descendants have crime and violence in common because they learned to defend themselves in the wrong way. They were never taught the right principles where they might have a father figure in a family who could teach them how to behave in society. They grew up in the streets without fears and feelings, so it is "normal" for them to behave in a way that is wrong for any kind of society. In this day and age, we all should learn how to behave nicely and live in a peaceful environment by teaching all kids how to do the same as they get older. If Haitians continue the violence and crime wherever they go, this will not only definitely give them a bad reputation, but they will never deserve any kind of respect as a human being in front of others.

Leadership Requirements

In 1954, a few years before I was born, Abraham Maslow (Maslow 1954) was putting together a hierarchical order for the needs of humans. His theory was actually based on healthy, creative people who were able to utilize their talents, potential, and capability. He mentioned in his writing that there are two major groups of human needs that he called *basic needs* and *meta needs*. For him, *basic needs* are physiological, such as food, water, and sleep, and psychological needs, such as affection, security, and self-esteem. Meta needs are more centered on others, because they focus on justice, goodness, beauty, order, and unity. Maslow argued that a person could not experience the meta needs without first having his or her *basic needs* met.

Leaders should be able to set direction, provide food and water for their citizens, and guide others to follow their direction, instead of telling them *"nage pou soti"* which means *"try to swim out of the ocean."* Haiti, a country created on the foundation of self-reliance in pursuit of prosperity, had fallen into a state of unrelieved despair (Rosenblum, 2009) "On February 5, Haitian president Rene Preval arrived in Washington carrying a desperate message in his pocket. In it, he requested emergency aid from the United States for as much as $100 million. Preval met with Secretary of State Hillary Clinton, officials at the World Bank and the International Monetary Fund, and congressional leaders" (Rosenblum, 2009). In fact, being a leader means being willing to take responsibility, since he or she is the main avenue to the development of an environment conducive to decision making. Leaders know that decision making should be their right as well as their responsibility. Leaders do not command excellence; they all have the ability to build excellence. In order to reach excellence, they must have good characters and morals and be imaginative. For example, they should show creativity by thinking of new ideas and solutions to problems, not begging around town.

They also have to be honest and trustworthy. They have to be fair-minded, broad-minded, and courageous by having the perseverance to accomplish a goal. How many leaders that have come and gone in Haiti since the day of independence until the present were able to reach the above criteria and have the qualities to be a leader? In fact, since the day of independence, they have failed to make any progress to develop the country.

The first man who declared independence for Haiti pronounced: "*Coupe tet, brule kay*," which means "cut all the heads and burn all of the houses." This was an insult to the country, because he passed a law allowing all citizens in the country to use violence by cutting necks and burning houses. Another reformer wrote during that period, "*il nou faut la peau d'un blanc pour parchemin, son crane pour ecritoire, son sang pour encre et une baionette pour plume*," which, translated into English, means: "They would need the skin of a white man for white paper, his blood for ink, his brain for the bottle that contains the ink, and a long knife for pen." Everyone can be proud of those who are against violence and crime and would not be able to tolerate this type of independence. In a country that has law, the funeral of these men would be celebrated in a prison cell, because what they proposed was considered attempted murder, which is punishable most of the time by a fifty-year sentence.

Rehabilitation of the Nation

Haiti is not ready for a presidential election. The country would need to change before its people can select anyone to be a leader, because all of the candidates are corrupt and ill-mannered as a result of the abuse they suffered. There is no way any of the candidates could be a good president, because they were abused in the past. The requirements to be a president are very complicated, and a candidate must have good character and morals; he should be able to solve problems, guide the nation in a better direction, be creative, and so on.

Haiti is a nation that has prepared everyone to be violent and criminal. Instead of having a presidential election and democracy, it would be preferable if they formed a national assembly that could sustain the nation while candidates are reformed and reeducated before coming to power. Based upon my experience and from what I have seen in my lifetime, the White House in Haiti is considered to be a "National Behavioral Palace Center," where it housed and continues to house all the mentally disabled gang patients who have not been treated by medical doctors and medications.

Furthermore, doctors at that behavioral center are never available, because all of them are always on permanent vacation. That was the main reason why all of the patients who were there from 1804 until the present time were distressed with all kinds of diseases. In addition, some of those mentally disabled gang members were like sacrificed kids, their souls buried alive within themselves. The Haitian White House is a place to sell drugs, engage in prostitution, commit crime, rape, kidnap, abuse alcohol, destroy property, rob, and threaten citizens. They have had more unreported diagnostic cases than that inside there.

This behavioral center might need to have its doctors in place in order to find a cure for its residents. After being treated at the behavioral palace center, they probably would be able to find one of its leaders or residents who would be able to speak on the situation. From this point on, the whole history of those leaders should be that they be considered patients because they are unable to meet the standards of proper functioning. In addition to that, it is the first behavioral center that has an official policy where its patients can voluntarily spend four years there and then leave at anytime without ever having had adequate treatment.

Health-Care Reform

Health care is considered an emergency for the nation because they have doctors, but they do not have hospitals, equipment, or medications, and their doctors are not really trained. Haitians are very innocent and naïve: they call a building a hospital because they have no other names available for it. In fact, it is not a hospital at all. Let us face the reality of what kinds of hospitals they have and what kinds of services are offered. First, in all of their "hospitals," they have no gloves to prevent transmission of germs, no garbage cans to properly dispose of normal and biohazardous waste, no emergency rooms for immediate treatment of critical injuries, no lights to see or electricity for what little equipment they do have, no private rooms for patients, no laboratory systems for analysis, no X-ray machines, no MRIs, no CAT scans or any other form of nuclear or radiological services for the diagnoses of the patients, and no nighttime doctors available for emergencies.

They only have dextrose IVs available for any patients that are sick, regardless of whether they are "Hyperglycemic". Also, nurses are not there to help the patients. They depend on the patient's family to clean and change the patient's bed. They are only there to pass out medications and wait for their shifts to end so they can leave.

Doctors are available only if you are really in need of one, and you might need to pay whatever money that he might ask on the spot. For example, suppose that your wife is pregnant, ready to give birth, and you are in need of an emergency room doctor. When the doctor arrives, you would have to pay him first before any treatment could be started. He would deliver the baby but not remove the placenta on purpose so that your wife might get an infection. Then he can make additional money off of you. This is a terrible situation!

Therefore, it seems that Haiti is really in need of health-care reform and the development of an adequate health-care system. The system needs to change its direction in order to integrate services more fully and offer quality services to the entire population in an equitable and efficient manner. Then they must rethink the roles and functions of the new system, because the old system is neither practical nor acceptable.

Although disease and health care are not independent phenomena, one cannot be reduced to the absence of the other. Illness is not the opposite of health. When a population lives longer, this does not mean that individuals are less ill. Longevity is accompanied by a change in the incidence and prevalence of various types of diseases and causes of mortality, not the elimination of illness.

It would appear that the ministry of health would need to place several psychiatric units in hospitals around the country to meet the needs of Haitian citizens. This refocusing of the health-care system, especially on mental illness, should be necessary in order to reconsider the integration of care and to provide security for all. The government and others from around the world who are willing to help have no other choice but to significantly restructure to the health-care system, which in turn would be able to reduce the violence and crimes. It would most likely have a positive influence on the social order in the broader sense of the term, indirectly but significantly. Hopefully with that, Haiti could well bring peace and enjoyment to the Caribbean nations, and everyone around the world would live in peace and enjoyment.

Medical Practice

As science and technology have been fully developed, medicine became more dependent upon medication. It is contrary in our country not only because the level of corruption is too high, but we don't have any medication available for any patient at the hospital. Also, the pharmacists are selling false medications; we have a system where everyone is trying to make money off of others. Most of the time, we use trickery to survive because we are unable to do the right thing.

Again, doctors at any hospital should assess their patients upon arrival by using clinical judgment. They begin their examination by learning about the patient's medical history (medical interview). They must have medical devices like stethoscopes, endoscopes, blood pressure cuffs, thermometers, etc. Most of Haiti's hospitals are empty because they have no basic medical equipment. We also have a major problem in our country where we have had no separate specialist doctors that can handle each patient accordingly since our time of independence. As we all know, "medicine" and "surgery" are two different categories, because "medicine" refers to the practice of nonoperative medicine, and most subspecialties in this area require preliminary training in "internal medicine." "Surgery" refers to the practice of operative medicine, and most subspecialties in this area require preliminary training in "general surgery." "Surgical training in the U.S. requires a minimum of five years of residency after medical school" (Author, 2004). In Haiti, it is different because everything is for sale. As long as you have money, you can absolutely buy any job even if you are a shoemaker. The government staff can employ you as a chief doctor at the hospital without any educational background.

It is also intended as an assurance and as a protection to every Haitian citizen to be against "charlatans" that usually practice inadequate medicine for personal gain. Also, doctors who are intentionally harmful should face charges of medical malpractice and should be subject to civil, criminal, or professional sanctions. Since we have been an independent country for centuries, it would be triumphant to see our orthopedic surgeons start to use medical devices, because they have been using knives and hammers to operate on their patients without any anesthesia. Since we have been an independent nation we should try to show our pride. We should research humanitarian medical suppliers and health care organizations that could provide the proper equipment and staff needed to bring the hospitals and clinics up to acceptable standards. Moreover, if you are unable to do this you might consider calling Home Depots in the United States. I would recommend that they contact them via phone in order to see if they can order some supplies like a jigsaw that would be able to operate on the patients faster than a knife because it is rude and cruel to use hammer and a knife. Some of us are unable to hear the sound in the place where patients suffer.

Moreover, many funeral homes in Haiti should also prearrange with the hospital staff to obtain clients because they rely on them. In fact, the hospital staffs make their commission on patients who are admitted, they are using all of their techniques to get you to the funeral home. The patient's charts are already transferred to the funeral home before the death. At this point, the funeral home would give them an injection to kill them. Shame on us! For me, the funeral home's role should be arranging funeral plans, securing necessary permits for death certificates, care and custody of the body, coordinating all details with the clergy, assisting arrangements for cemetery space, grave opening and closing, flowers and so forth, instead of trying to buy bodies to make profit. In a country that has laws, the hospital staff and the funeral home owner should be placed in prison for murder, and they should definitely be on a death row waiting list.

Based upon my experience, no one is safe in Haiti. As a result, crime in Haiti is a business and a habit; it becomes part of the Haitian culture. Then again, Aristotle notes: "it may be difficult for an individual to become virtuous if he or she has not acquired the habit of acting virtuously" (Bostock, 2000). In order for the nation to remove this criminality habit, I would suggest they automatically remove the name of the nation in their mentality that has the meaning of "hate yourself" which is considered the meaning of Haiti and we need to spiritually transform it on "love yourself" because we are not the devil's or Lucifer's descendants.

Philosophical Inquiry

It would be a great adventure to see all the slave descendants around the world start to behave normally like human beings, treating their brothers and sisters with respect and dignity, and treating themselves with respect as well. It will also be a glory to start seeing them respect and obey the laws. It would be considered a great achievement to preserve the rule of peace through all areas of the Republic of Haiti.

It would be very naïve to require courage, participation, and imagination without fixed rules, regulations, and without placing strong sanctions on the Republic. Jean-Jacques Rousseau, an ancient philosopher, in his early writing contended in his "social contract" that "the progress of knowledge had made governments more powerful and crushed individual liberty" (Rousseau, 1762b). His most important work describes the relationship of man with society. He also mentioned in his political philosophy that politics and morality should be one. In Haiti's case, we have had several leaders who have pretended to be politicians and had no morals; they acted as ancient slaves without any educational background. At the end of his philosophical writing, Rousseau mentioned that all the politicians and the leaders should put in applications and pass them from generation to generation: "plants are shaped by cultivation and men by education. We are born weak, we need strength; we are born totally unprovided for, we need aid; we are born stupid, we need judgment. Everything we do not have at our birth and which we need when we are grown is given us by education (Rousseau, 1762a).

I strongly feel that Haiti might have a better outlook if its entire population were educated to the maximum of their ability, because a highly educated workforce is good for the economy of any country. A strong commitment to education would also attract foreign investment. They usually have in their mind: *"qui embrace trop mal etreint"* which means in English, "whoever holds too many will have hard times to hold them." This particular phrase has paralyzed their minds to where all they think about is that one will go crazy if he studies too many things at the same time. Today I can attest that that phrase is wrong, because more qualifications are a positive development.

Army Reform

To the best of my knowledge, in the past, we had an army in the Republic that was malformed and was not adequately educated. Let us forget about the past and look at the future to ensure the security of the future generation. At this point, as we all can testify, there is no country in the world that can provide stability, defense, and security without the presence of the army except for a country that is well developed. The military is a support to the nation; it plays an important role in any society. Therefore, I should address the creation of professional army officers with adequate and better institutions in order to secure the lives of citizens and visitors in the country.

It has always been said that Costa Rica does not have an army, but they are not of the same quality as Haiti. The Costa Ricans are more cultivated and more civilized educationally. They are considered the most literate population in Central America. In 1994, President Figueres advocated a computer in each school district. The nation has four thousand schools, and students are not required to pay for assistance. The literacy rate in Costa Rica is 96 percent according to the *CIA World Fact Book*. The official government estimate, based on the 2004 Census, shows a value of 74.3 percent (2005), growing at 0.1 percent per year (Central Department of Statistics).

Moreover, Haiti should form an administration in which the citizens would live under the law, obey it with respect and dignity, and always maintain good character and morals in order to continue this service. The country's administration would need to treat every citizen with respect and protect the rights of the citizens in the country. If any officials participate in any type of criminal activities, they must be judged and prosecuted as any civil criminals, because no one is exempt from the rules, regulations, and strong sanctions. Justice is for everyone, and there is no exception, whether they are the children of a general, a governor, or a president.

Then again, anyone that carries a weapon in this world should understand the importance of it. It is not a toy with which to play, show power, or destroy human beings. Weapons are created for defensive purposes, to protect soldiers in wartime and also to protect anyone against violence. In fact, Haitians are using these weapons wrongly in their country just to fight and kill others. This is an act of insanity, because no one person has the right to take away the life of another. Thus, we understand that there is a mental component that suggests that the ones carrying the weapons are not truly qualified to use them. As such, they would not be allowed by law to have them. In the past, they used knives to kill anyone at any time. From generation to generation, their mindset has always been all about killing. I am writing this book to put a stop to it, because Haitians are really in need of psychiatric help, and if they get that, we can look forward to positive changes in the future.

Origin of Violence

It seems that this particular mechanism comes from the ancestry in Haiti. I remember when I was fifteen years old; Jean-Claude Duvalier was the president of Haiti. One of his *tonton macoutes* had brought a "zombie" to the police station. At that time, the president requested that the colonel of the police department bring the zombie to the palace.

It is very easy to transform someone into a zombie based on what I have seen in the past and how I understand the process. A zombie can definitely stay in the same condition until he or she eats salts or meat. Several years ago, a voodoo priest who was working for the American Sugar Company in Haiti had several workers working at the same field, and all of those workers were zombies. He took the money that they received and fed them only unsalted foods. A portion of the puffer fish is usually used to make someone a zombie. It is one of the strongest nerve poisons available. The clinical drug Norcuron has the same effect, but it is only used during surgery.

The puffer fish causes severe neurological damage to the left side of the brain. The left side of the brain controls speech, memory, and motor skills. During that period of time, you never heard any other history in Haiti. Thomas Von Harrington on zombie secrets states, "It shall also be qualified as attempted murder the employment which may be made against any person of substances which, without causing actual death, produce a lethargic coma more or less prolonged. If, after the person had been buried, the act shall be considered murder no matter what result follows" (Von Harrington (2002) To be honest with you, those zombies were numerous during my adolescence, and every kid at that time was afraid to make friends, share ideas, and communicate to each other. You might say something at that time that would be enough to make you become a zombie; therefore, how would you expect to get along with others when you might go a long time without any relationships because of the fear of zombies?

The zombie industry is formally created for Haitian businesses, because some business owners have the idea that they do not need to work themselves if they have some zombies to do it for them. For example, you might have some land and you need to plant food. Who are you going to find to do all of the work when everyone thinks those are dirty jobs reserved for nonprofessional men? Therefore, they all try to find some guys in the street who will curse someone and transform that person to a zombie class, where the voodoo priest can then rent that person out for one dollar per day. Sometimes business owners buy their own team of zombies from other voodoo priests so they can make their own money hiring out zombies. Every day, these voodoo exploiters try to "recruit" more zombies so they can make more money. That is the way most of them function, and they are still doing it to the present time. This kind of violence is caused by low socioeconomic status, urban residency, low intelligence, and poor skills. According to President Kennedy, I think that it is not only useful to point out something when it needs pointing out, but when it comes to destructive, divisive behavior and speech, I think that it is an absolute obligation to do so" (Kennedy, 1966).

Further, school in Haiti contains more violence than you can imagine. You would need to be the girlfriend of the professors before you could even think about finishing school; otherwise, you will not make it. There was one professor that pronounced to a student, "*kimbe coco oua mange caca,*" which, in so many words means that if you do not let me have sex with you, you will live your life in the streets, because you will not get any grade to pass the class, and without education you might wind up being displeased with your life. The literal translation of this phrase is, "hold your vagina, then you will eat shit."

Another personal example of the source of violence happened to me when I was in high school. One of my professors wanted to be in love with me. At that time, I was sixteen years old, and he sent me a letter to come to meet him at his clinic; he was a doctor. I took the letter and gave it to my parents. I do not know what happened; my parents sent it to the Department of Education where that professor was connected with the *tonton macoutes* in Haiti. He did not lose his job because he was so powerful. In return, I had a problem with him not wanting me in the classroom while he was teaching. Therefore, I studied outside of class with my classmates to be ready for exams, and I finally finished high school.

This forced me to be my own teacher, which also gave me the opportunity to think about leaving the country one day. This was the best decision I ever made, because that helped develop my independence and gave me a strong character, so that even if I failed, I would still know how to succeed again. As a result, with my experience of observing how American teachers operate, I do not believe there are any Haitians who are prepared to be a teacher or professor in America. In reality, with time, I finally have a better life than what I would have had in Haiti, because I was forced to learn independence from a cruel Haitian professor. Without that experience, I do not believe I could have reached where I am today.

Domestic Violence

The right and formal name for domestic violence is domestic abuse, spousal abuse, or partner violence. Most of the time, it occurs when one of the Haitians is trying to dominate another; this is the way it has happened in our environment. As far as I know, it has occurred in all cultures, ethnicities, religions, sexes, classes, etc. Realistically, it has many forms in addition to physical violence; for example, emotional abuse, intimidation, economic deprivation, and threats of violence. It is perpetrated by both men and women where most of the time it is considered a criminal offense and physical assault. Emotionally, most of the Haitian women like to be sexually assaulted by their partner because they believe they are loved only when they are beaten. Most Haitian men are proud when they beat their wives or partners because that is the only way they can feel superior. Without beating and raping in Haiti, there is no guarantee that "love" would still exist. "An important component of domestic violence, often ignored, is the realm of passive abuse, leading to violence. Passive abuse is covert, subtle, and veiled. This includes victimization, procrastination, forgetfulness, ambiguity, neglect, spiritual, and intellectual abuse" (Author, 2009). Psychologically, most of Haiti's women should be evaluated by a professional psychiatrist and follow treatment because those needs are essentially important for the safety of everyone that is around. "Arthritis, hypertension, and heart disease have been identified by battered women as directly caused or aggravated by domestic violence suffered early in their adult lives" (Clark County Prosecuting Attorney, 2009). Then again, Olga Fagan, on the history of violence and rape that is common in Haiti, said, "it is an uphill battle, with gang rape more common because of the proliferation of arms and drugs. SOFA sees two main issues: the incidence of domestic violence and incest and the increase in gang rapes. In a recent report published by SOFA it was estimated that eight out of every ten women suffer domestic violence and the incidence of rape is increasing." He also mentions that, "Many of the gangsters are on drugs and roam the cities and countryside seeking thrills, often targeting women who live alone" (Fagan, 2006).

For as long as we have been an independent country, we should put in our mind that everyone should be born free and equal in dignity and rights. Each of us should have the right to be protected by law against such abuse or attacks. "Along with depression, domestic violence victims may also experience Post-traumatic Stress Disorder (PTSD), which is characterized by symptoms such as flashbacks, intrusive imagery, nightmares, anxiety, emotional numbing, insomnia, hypervigilance, and avoidance of traumatic triggers" (Vitanza, Vogel, and Marshall, 1995).

In addition to that, most Haitian parents also sexually abuse their children at puberty because they spiritually need the blood of the first-born child for good luck, basically they need a virgin. The voodoo priest, most of the time, asks the parent to get the blood or he might ask the mother to bring her daughter with her. In one case, I literally witnessed a beautiful little girl who became his wife, and this particular one used to sleep with the youngest girl because most of the voodoo priests think that this would be the only way to appeal their demand rapidly toward Lucifer. This is a fact, not a myth!

Again, most of our mothers who are pious towards Catholicism are afraid and very sensitive when their daughters have reached the age of puberty, because they are also afraid they are at risk to lose their communion at the church. They always do their test by using a chicken egg and forcing it to see if it can get into the vagina to make sure their girls are not sexually active. This test is always done every month during puberty until they are ready to be married. If they discover that you are sexually active, they will take a piece of wood that is burning and place it into the vagina permanently chastising the child. This incident has happened many times while I was growing up. The victims were about thirteen to fourteen years old. One of them is still alive, but the other committed suicide the same day by drinking a bottle of mosquito repellant. I really condemn this form of test, because it is considered psychological abuse, and my recommendation would be to have a department placed for children and families and adult protective services to record and correct future abuse.

Confession

I sincerely write this message in order to guide the nation in a better direction. I do not have any intention of accepting any position in the country, because I have already changed my nationality. According to my American constitution, I must obey all the rules and the regulations, and I am dedicated to do so. I would not be able to engage myself in any political way in another country. My message is intended to serve as guidance for reform for those who would be able to work within Haiti to change its perspective on its society.

My personality and my morals that I have developed in my new nation will keep me safe and secure enough to achieve anything that I may decide to do in the future. I am very happy comparing the way that I was treated before coming to the United States. I had a chance to come and start a new life in which I can exploit all the opportunities that this land has offered me instead of being exploited by others. I went to college and earned a degree, and even as I write this book I am pursuing my PhD. I have been treated fairly in this country without any prejudice. I have never been discriminated against for any reason since the day that I came here.

I have been all over the country moving from one place to another. I am a very creative and curious person who likes to learn about and visit other places. I have learned and matured greatly from my experiences, including how to adapt to change. The experience has also changed my behavior, culture, social activities, education, and so forth. Coming to the United States has really served as guidance in my life, teaching me new skills in order to be able to live wherever I might choose in the future.

I am very happy with the new skills that I have acquired in America; it is a powerful country filled with many opportunities; it has totally changed my entire personality and made me a new person. From where I came from and the way I had been taught, I have confidence that they have done a good job for me. Now I am proud and feel I should share all those good ideas with all my brothers and sisters who are slave descendants. I believe if I can change, we all should be able to change, because it is not too hard to do so.

My concepts are no big secret; the trick is that you have to be willing to learn, to follow directions, and to read instructions about everything before you do anything. You can also choose to imitate, since imitation is a natural phenomena in civilization, and it is the highest form of flattery. When I say imitate, I mean imitate the good side, not the bad side. Finally, we must live under the law; part of our jobs would be to obey it.

Communication

As we all know, communication plays an integral role in any society. It is considered one of the most important skills that anyone in any country can have in business, politics, at home, at school, or even in life. I believe we will live happier lives and become more productive if we can improve our ability to communicate.

In Haiti, communication doesn't exist for many reasons. First of all, with the practice of voodoo, everyone is afraid to speak to one another, because some of them are afraid of becoming zombies. Second, some of them are also afraid because of political concerns. In addition, a small percentage of them are Catholic, and they do not want to talk to Protestants or Baptists. Also, some of them think they are so rich they cannot talk to others, because they think the others might be poor. Sometimes they finished high school thinking they could not communicate with illiterates, which makes communication very tough in that little country.

Since they are one nation, I believe they should unify as one nation. In contrast, they have been divided into different groups and classes, which makes it worse for themselves and others. Part of their problem is the division of the classes, which creates more complexities. Kids are unable to speak with their own parents; if they take a chance and open their mouths to say something, their parents would beat them or tie them in a chair all day as a punishment. The parents used to say: "*fout bouda yon kote lan med*," which means, "put your buttocks somewhere, fuck you." This is a sad situation! Without a way of communicating and getting along with others, they may face hard times in accomplishing their democratic plan, because none of them have been properly prepared for that form of government in their lifetimes.

Beyond that, communication is a successful plan for any country when the sender and the receiver are able to understand the same information. In Haiti, no one is allowed to speak, because they are unable to understand each other. They all are very argumentative. All human beings are born with the ability to vocalize, but many in Haiti lack the knowledge, attitudes, and skills that would truly define communication competence. However, the ability to communicate can only be learned, and it can only be taught at home and at school. A minimum of discipline should enhance relations with others in the society, making communication central to general education requirements. According to Bruskin and Goldring, in *Communication Education*, "It should be included in early childhood education and should continue through adult education, because it would improve specific skills and abilities like critical thinking, media skills, literacy and criticism, leadership skills, and family relational development" (Bruskin and Goldring, 1993). In fact, oral communication is so important that it can contribute to all our social adjustment and participation and satisfy our interpersonal relationships.

Freedom

The reality of freedom is preserved by free people: if you have never been free, then you would remain a slave or prisoner wherever you are in the world. Generally speaking, the quality of a nation is judged by the size of its educated population. Without education, you would never be able to achieve growth and development, and most importantly, you would never be able to sustain it.

You are dead wrong, my Haitian brothers and sisters, if you think that you are free. You are not free when the police are always looking for you. If you get caught by the police, you will not be free: if you are at home, you also are not free. You were free only on the day that you were born. As you grew older, your freedom was reduced little by little without your knowledge. In fact, education has an immense impact on human society. The knowledge and information that are spreading around the world come through education. In a broader sense, we are all animals, but we will transform and become rational animals only through education.

Moreover, why has the United States been the richest and most developed country and nation in the world for an era? It has a very high literacy rate and productive human resources. It also has selective training and education to meet any technological and business demands for future generations. Generally speaking, the importance of education should not be neglected by anyone, because it is an absolute necessity for the economic and social development of any nation. An investment in education is also associated with a higher probability of employment.

Since knowledge is a sacred duty, I come to my final point, that living without knowledge and education is little more than existence. You are not living because you are not free when you imprison yourselves and are unable to speak, think, and do what you want. This is especially tragic given the new technology that everyone is using to communicate with each other.

Peace

Since peace is a psychological comfort, you Haitians might need to create a way to start bringing more peace to the country, because no one can live without it. There is no way you would be able to function properly without it. Living with all of the fears that have been created in the country will eventually cause its residents to become mentally disabled or imbalanced. There would be more suicide cases in the country, and the lack of peace would also cause more stress and depression.

I am grateful to President John F. Kennedy for having developed an agency of the federal government that has been devoted to world peace and friendship. He was the first one in 1960 who started this plan, which today has many volunteers in support of it. According to Theodore M. Vestal (2001), "After winning the presidency, one of Kennedy's first acts was to establish the president's task force on the Peace Corps. He chose his brother-in-law, R. Sargent Shriver, to head the task force and to report to him on how the Peace Corps could be organized, and then to organize it." In fact, there are 190,000 Peace Corps volunteers around the world who are available for any issue, from AIDS education to information technology to environmental preservation. They have also helped school children develop computer skills.

We must give credit to President George W. Bush for continuing this excellent project. He said in a speech: "We are exploring all options as to how to keep the situation peaceful and stable" Lou Dobbs at CNN (2003). In spite of that, he made a decision to create Homeland Security after September 11, 2001, for the benefit of the citizens, to protect the American people, and to disrupt terrorist attacks. All of those decisions were made to ensure that everyone would be safe and have peace of mind in the country.

In contrast, the country of Haiti has been overwhelmed by peace-hating leaders who have so much power that they have corrupted nearly every citizen, thus giving Haiti the name "country of the devils." In fact, everyone has been practicing this nonsense for so long a period of time; I can only tell you that they have done a great job. And I can tell you today with a full guarantee that each Haitian home is not a real house; it is a psychiatric unit for each family, without any medication or doctor. Their practices are fully and totally wrong, regardless of what they think they might feel they have achieved and accomplished in their lives.

Since the principle role of a leader is not just an abstract exercise, he or she must have the leadership skills, potential, and knowledge to exercise the autonomy and authority necessary in order to pursue these strategies. They all are unable to prove to me or anyone else that they can perform as leaders when they do not have any proof of such abilities. I would like to see all of them taking the necessary actions to stop the violence, improve security, bring more happiness, and establish peace in each corner of the country. They need to make it a priority to move the country that they are living in toward a better future plan.

Voodoo power should be able to help Haiti build a sense of unity, since it is the only supernatural power that they have used in their entire lives. This particular power at this time could be utilized to harness the enthusiasm, participation, and courage of its citizenry, just as it was in Cuba as I mentioned above. It is important to that country because they all are sincerely in need of its forceful presence in a situation like that. If they have encountered any difficulties to solve all of those problems, they would be the only ones who could take the blame or the credit for the outcomes of their actions and policies.

Food Sanitation

Sanitation is a way of life. Everyone should be aware that they must live in a clean environment in order to be healthy. We all know that most diseases are contracted at birth from dirt. A sanitation program is only as good as the attitude, willingness, and efforts of people. Cleanliness is the most important sanitation program. The country does not even have a local health department anywhere. They are in urgent need of streets and sanitation and residential garbage pickup. They have no parking signs, no street sweeping, no trash compactor ordinance, no toilet paper, and no proper sanitation. It is incredible to see it that way!

Haiti is a country that has been independent since 1804, and its citizens are still relieving their bowels in the streets and cleaning themselves with leaves. In fact, if they are unable to reach leaves, they would rather clean themselves at the electric pole. Also they have developed the habit that most of them urinate wherever they can find. This is unacceptable in any country that desires either to be democratic or independent.

After a long period of being independent, they should have found a better way to dispose of garbage than burning. Burning garbage produces toxins that carry negative side effects or properties:

- benzene (leukemia)

- toluene diisocyanate (asthma)

- nitrogen oxides (lung)

- nitrite compounds (poisoning, cancer)

- hydrogen cyanide (respiratory difficulty)

- formaldehyde (nose and throat cancer, cardiovascular disease, diabetes).

The short-term illnesses might be like allergies: irritation of your eyes, nose, throat, lungs, as well as congestion. When burning papers, plastics with leftover foods, bottles, and so forth, you do not really destroy anything; you just change the chemical form. The bad news about burning anything is that you just do not know what the resulting pollutant will be. Today, scientists have discovered that burning garbage also causes global warming, which in turn damages the atmosphere. It would be very kind to everyone if we could all put our heads together to plan a better future for Haiti and live pleasantly on the earth.

Another important factor for the citizens of Haiti is that they have been eating nonfood items. "This results in negative consequences and may cause developmental disorders, such as mental retardation, or pervasive developmental disorders to newborns." In addition, "there is also evidence that supports the usefulness of the flora found in soil. Some have even suggested that it is useful, if not vital, in the establishment of healthy bacteria within the digestive tract, addressing the problems presented by Crohn's Disease and Leaky Gut Syndrome. Highly adsorbent families of clays have been demonstrated to cause the lining of the vertebrate gut to change both on a cellular and a cellular level, potentially protecting the gut from chemical insults as well as alleviating ailments such as esophagitis, gastritis, and colitis" (Henry and Kwong, 2003). In fact, "the international classification of disease includes geophagia among eating disorders as a variety of pica, which is considered as the ingestion of nonfoods. Further, there is evidence that supports the ability of the flora found in soil that will damage toothenamel" (Henry Jacques and Alicia M. Kwong, (2003) p. 355). Also, some unwittingly ingest a variety of bacteria leading to poisoning and intestinal obstruction. Rising food prices in Haiti had driven many Haitians to consume dirt cookies on a regular basis to ward off hunger, thereby absorbing dangerous toxins.

Moreover, selling foods on a dirt floor is considered the most serious danger there. Anyone can relieve their bowels on the floor, and another one stops at the same spot to sell food. That is really a scandal for a country that really wants to become democratic and wants to keep its independence. It is a shameful situation to know about it, because it is considered a violation of confidentiality. In reality, as a humanitarian, it would be a crime if I know it is wrong and do nothing to help this situation. They need serious rules and regulations on food selling, because most Haitians are buying and eating microbes.

It is also a sad situation to look at a seller with uncovered open cuts or wounds. They should not handle food unless the injury is completely protected by a secure, waterproof covering. Also chewing tobacco and smoking cigarettes and pipes should not permitted in food handling areas. Finally, they should have an office of pest control in the country since they have many restaurants and food storage facilities in the country. Effective pest control program should be verified on a regular basis. "Community hygiene is an important part of public health that most doctors know about and they all have treated cases of food poisoning at some time in their lives, besides treating cases in their patients" (LSU Law Center, 2009).

Secret of Feces

There is a voodoo secret about feces in Haiti, because feces play an integral role for the religion. The reason I mention it is because feces is involved in anything that Haitians plan to do. First of all, voodoo priests make a compound that involves the first feces of the newborns with their burned umbilical cords, and includes nutmeg, mascriti oil, and castor oil. They put all of those ingredients in one teaspoon and give it to the babies to swallow.

Second if the people have a restaurant, they must cook with the mixture of the feces in order to have more customers every day. Moreover, both men and women use "bowel tea" for their partners in order to keep their partner forever; in this case, the "bowel tea" is called *tu voudras,* a term that means "you will want." A man or woman who is willing to stay with his or her spouse will always have a tendency to use this voodoo secret. They swallow a whole nutmeg, and then look for it when relieving the bowels. Then they take it with a little piece of feces and make a cinnamon tea with it, and their partners will never be able to leave them. I truly believe that voodoo priests should be placed in psychiatric facilities for inventing those compounds for all their clients.

Generally speaking, anyone can become very sick by eating feces because they contain so many types of bacteria and parasites that can be very harmful to the human body. Those complications may involve hepatitis B and C, oral infection, abscess, and a variety of other infectious diseases; besides that, think about the morning breath!

According to Visualize Publishing LLC, many Haitians are malnourished and infected with parasitic worms as well Alecia Settle 2008 (Settle 2008). They live in a place without diapers or toilets. Barefoot children walk across soil contaminated with feces. Without running water to bathe, they can easily become infected. What little food they receive will not be fully used, because the parasites steal the nutrients. In a country with little access to medical care, they are not treated for sickness and disease, and the problem escalates.

Blood Drinking

Most Haitians, especially the groups that believe in voodoo, are considered to be vampires if they like to drink blood—not their own but someone else's. According to the articles "Haiti Makes Voodoo Official," "Haiti is reckoned as being 95% Christian (predominantly Catholic), but according to Catholic missionary John Hoet, Haitians 'are 100% voodoo.' Most are nominally Roman Catholic Christians, but most also practice some aspects of voodoo and incorporate Christian saints into their pagan pantheon of African gods. Haiti ended its official recognition of Roman Catholicism as its state church in 1987" (Williams, 2003).

According to historian Joel A. Ruth (2004), "Aristide reportedly supplied Clinton with a voodoo sorcerer. This sorcerer, according to the Haitian media, gave Clinton magical advice on how to run his campaign. One piece of advice that Clinton reportedly followed: not to change his underwear during the final week of the 1992 race." In addition to that, Aristide dedicated the ceremonial site prior to Clinton's arrival with "the blood of a newborn infant in gratitude to the gods whom he believes allowed his return to power." They especially like to "suck out babies' blood, which is atrocious, because babies can only cry when they are hurting. Babies are there to be eaten by these bloodsuckers, but they are unable to say anything and defend themselves" (Ponte, 2004).

This makes you even sicker when you believe that you are under the possession of the devil spirits. In the United States, I would bet that you are not able to take those risks since you know that the death penalty has a clean, polished seat waiting for you. Haitians have done everything to prove that they are not normal, which suggests that most Haitians should definitely live in a psychiatric unit to learn the difference between animals and human beings. I have never known and have never seen people drinking blood, eating people, and eating feces anywhere in the world except in Haiti. I would like to know when all of us will be able to put an end to nonsense. Regardless of how educated we are, it seems that there is no solution to our problems. My recommendation will finally be to place a psychiatric unit in our country to clean-up our Haitian's culture that is being devastated since our creation.

Again, what makes everyone angry about that is the fact that you do not even know what you are doing while you are drinking the blood. It is wrong for anyone to drink something that is pathogenic, yet Haitians cannot seem to tell the difference. Since the spirits are supernatural, they should be able to provide their students with all the skills and knowledge so that they know that they can catch several diseases such as hepatitis A, B, and C, HIV or AIDS, lupus, and STDs from drinking blood. How come the spirits cannot teach all of that? A federal recommendation to exclude certain Haitians from blood donations as a safeguard against spreading AIDS has been expanded to all Haitians, and the change is being protested by Haitian organizations in New York City and Miami.

During the year of 1986, we all were angry and ran a strike in front of the FDA building in Manhattan, New York. In fact, "Leaders of Haitian-American organizations, who say there are 150,000 Haitian immigrants and their relatives in the Miami area, and 350,000 in the New York area, say the policy is irrational because Haitians are no more likely to carry the AIDS virus than some other groups. The Haitian-American leaders also say the move will revive the stigma and bias that afflicted Haitians when the federal Centers for Disease Control initially listed them as a high-risk group." Lambert (1990). (Bruce Lambert 1990) All of us should give them credit for this particular declaration instead of blaming them because we all know that we are vampires. That declaration tells me that Americans have good laboratory and professional technicians to detect any disease. That also tells me that we are all secured by professionals with good hearts in the United States since they had never witnessed us drinking blood, but they can find the source of it. In fact, they had removed this classification on paper, but in their mind I believe it must still remain the same because their laboratory is still in function for clarification. Based upon my experience and what I had witnessed in my country, I can certainly testify today that they were right and we were wrong. I don't believe that they were wrong when they had made that declaration. I would like to ask each of you a favor: I would like you to become a nation with ethics by starting to have conscience, honesty, integrity, and personality. As everyone says, "the truth hurts." However, we must accept it. Without scientists, biologists and the Centers for Disease Control, we all would be buried by now because no one in Haiti thought to test the death blood before drinking, and we do not have any laboratories. A child might be born with AIDS then you sacrifice that child and drink his blood. I don't think it is proper when we are hiding facts because we must be honest to each other on this earth. Then again, how does a Haitian man find out if this child who is born belongs to him? In another sense, how do we usually do our DNA testing? We have been using the same technique since our creation by pulling blood from our finger and giving it to the newborn to drink. If the newborn doesn't belong to the person who gives him the blood to drink: he or she will die. This test is false based upon my experience, and you don't have any idea how many of them might die innocently because the blood might contain several diseases. This "test belief" is forcibly wrong my brothers and sisters! Moreover, we know that we are a nation with full revenge that will pass this disease around maliciously as soon as we find out that we obtained it from someone.

It is unreal for supernatural powers not to know what we all need down here, because they belong to another world. They can travel from their world to come to earth any time they want, yet they are unable to teach a little thing that anyone who does not live according to his potential can explain. These spirits are not real, because they are also uneducated the same way as their students or clients. Today with the advances in technology, if those spirits and their students continue to drink blood it is because either the spirits, evil ones, Satan, or the students are all insane. All of them should be locked in a psychiatric hospital under medical care to receive treatment because all of them are out of their minds.

Black Debate

Since we Haitians are the only group in the world who are complaining that the white man is a racist, today we are forming a debate in order to justify the complaint in a formal and logical manner. Do you think if the Americans, Canadians, and others were so racist that they would let you come live in their countries? They have taken their time to build an embassy in each country in the world to invite anyone to come to their country. As a result, you have declared that they are racist. Do you think that they are still racist, yes or no? In fact, many who have come to America seem to have come in order to break their laws, because they are unable to behave as human beings in the society. By law, they are allowed to arrest anyone who is misbehaving and throw them in prison. In prison, they are prepared to give you the skills and training you need so that you may learn how to behave inside a prison cell. Once you have served your time and learned your lesson, you will be prepared to live in society without any other problems.

Second, our habits are very rare. We do not like to work, and we prefer to sleep all day and night, eat all day, have sex all day and night, and steal all the time. Most of us are afraid to learn and are unable to accept schooling. Psychologically, do you think with behavior like that, that anyone would appreciate us? There is no reason for us to behave in the way many of us are behaving right at this moment.

Moreover, if the Americans were really racists, they would never have elected Barack Obama to become a presidential candidate or to have elected him to the highest office of the land. Condoleezza Rice would not have been chosen to work at the White House. General Colin Powell would not have retired from the military to take a White House job. Others who are black would never be in their positions. That means racism does not exist corporately in America, but it exists on an individual level for the one who is impure in the society.

It is very hard to live without peace. There is no one who would be able to function without peace. We are a burden to the society when we always create a negative impact on society. We have lived in the same way and with the same way of thinking since slavery, and we never change. Today we believe that everyone should tolerate us with our wild life being something that all of us have in common. When will we change and have an ethical aspect that would earn us all a minimum of respect? It is absolutely necessary to live that way, because human beings should treat themselves as human beings, not as animals. We are treating ourselves as animals; this is the reason others are afraid of us. Some of us that choose to be treated as human beings are welcomed by Americans.

Again, we need to be more pleasant with people. It seems that we never learned about discipline, politeness, good manners, kindness, and so on. All of us need to calm down and think about it, because it is not normal to misbehave all the time. Wherever we come from—Africa, Haiti, England, France, and all over the world—blacks have these things in common: brutality, stealing, aggressive behavior, cheating, criminal behavior, violence, and so on. Those behaviors did not come from the slavery. You would need to do research to find out from where those behaviors come, because they are not acceptable. Regardless of whether I am white or black, I would not be able to digest this type of nonsensical behavior. It is about time to change and try the best we can to see if we can have another image in the environment. We were not the only slaves on this earth. In the beginning, everyone was a slave: white, black, Japanese, Philippine, Jewish, and so on. We are the only ones who are distinguished in the group. What makes us look different? Our education and our behavior separate us even from people who belong to the same group as we do. We need to think about that, my brothers and sisters.

Furthermore, labor is a social responsibility where it opens doors to freedom. Most of us like to sleep during the daytime after lunch. Adam I. Qureshi, Assistant Professor of Neurology, affiliated with the University of Buffalo's Toshiba Stroke Research Center, found that "excessive daytime sleepiness should be assessed for depression, obesity, and diabetes." (Qureshi , 2008). He also advised that individuals who snore severely or have trouble staying awake during the day should see a doctor to find out why. These symptoms may be a sign of sleep apnea, which is associated with an increased risk of having a stroke. In fact, sleeping can probably be a sign of depression. As we all know, depression is one part of bipolar disorder which is part of mental illness. That means all of us are sick. This is incredible!

Finally, everyone who went in the past to those voodoo priests also had sexual relationships with their voodoo priests. The priests told them that would be the only way that the spirit might come; it is by having the sperm that tells everyone the sperm would be gladly needed in those cases. The voodoo industry is not only made for the spirit; it also involves sexual abuse, homosexuality, lesbians, crime, and kidnappings as well. If you refuse anything for any reason you might not have a chance to go back from where you came. They are also cannibals, and they have the option to eat anyone that comes in front of them. They cook people like any chicken in Haiti. Most of them usually say that human bodies have a better taste than animal meats. Part of their belief system involves eating a human being so they can become stronger spiritually. Stopping this nonsense would play an integral role in reducing the crime and violence around Haiti.

Ethics of the Nation

Misconduct and unethical behaviors take control of the situation because the Haitians are unable to discern the difference between right and wrong. Part of the nation's culture is violence and crime. With that, it would be very difficult to establish an ethical and moral aspect in a country where most of its citizens are illiterate and mentally sick. A moral identity is the sense that certain core virtues are essential in any country. It is considered the key part of constructive leadership. Generally speaking, no one needs to be educated in order to have moral identity, and for that purpose there is no question about the color of skin.

Ensuring integrity, ethics, personality, and morals would automatically promote the value of the nation. At this present time, the nation has no value since its inhabitants are mostly involved in crime and violence, and the country cannot provide any form of security for any citizen from around the world. Therefore, a system of ethics would need to be put in place where everyone around the world who has their family in Haiti may have peace of mind when they are away from their loved ones. It is really considered a crisis to see how most of the black Haitians are behaving around the world.

It is also a sad situation to see that most blacks are living with no hope, no ambition, and no love for anyone. They all are afraid of each other; they do not even trust their own families. I really do not understand what is going on right now, because I do not see any reason why people cannot get along with each other. We are really fortunate to have a pleasant earth surrounded by different plants, a nice ocean for cruising around the world, and nice animals to eat every day. Why would a nation put itself in a situation where its residents are killing each other for no reason? They create their own war that will never end without the help of others.

Cultural Diversity

Today, we would need to do a reform by replacing the centuries-old notion of violence and crime with education, development, and civilization of the nation. We all around the world can work together to bring diversity and success, since diversity is sharing values. In the sixteenth century, the meaning of the word *cultivating* was "forming and shaping the mind." In another sense, culture represents the values and beliefs that can determine how we all can put our heads together to do things and how we must structure our ways of thinking. We would need to concentrate work in the economic and infrastructure development, and in the education of the country to have a chance of bringing success to future generations.

Moreover, the basics of life should not be violence, crime, drugs, and sex. It should be a constitutional birthright where each citizen is free to live without fear and anxiety. We also need to concentrate on a humanist culture by learning to contribute to the development of judgment and sensibility. I would like each of us to start to understand the meaning of unity, diversity, civilization, and societies. We should always remember that human organization is based on a code of conduct that should be respected: we need to work in groups, because working in a group certainly involves shared and learned values. Without that, there is no guarantee that Haitians will succeed and be able to lead a successful life in society.

Furthermore, I have read in the newspaper that the nation is crying out for food. Any government around the world should be able to ensure adequate capacity for all basic needs by creating jobs for every citizen in the country. There is no way that anyone can reach their highest potential if they are unable to have food to eat, a house to live in, clothes, healthcare, education, and security. The cultural diversity in the country is the greatest need for its citizens. I have visited many countries in the past where I have not seen so many of these problems. Generally speaking, a need for education and a mental institution should be able to change the face of the country by giving its citizens a different outlook as compared to present time.

Again, life in society should be based on self-respect, respect for others, respect for the opposite sex, and respect for privacy. We all are in need of that, especially in the slave culture. We also need to desire to resolve conflicts peacefully and remember there is no man that can exist without others. We need to develop a sense of responsibility toward others in the sense of solidarity. Another important thing to know is the distinction between professional, public, and private life. Learning to communicate and work in groups means being able to listen and negotiate. If you are willing to try my advice, you should be able to live without fear and anxiety. It would not be an obligation; it would be only a choice, since everyone has a right to choose what they want.

Finally, I suggest that everyone try to understand the needs of Haiti by simply disregarding and forgiving its citizens' behavior and their manner, because they are really innocent and not aware of their sense of insanity. They are very uneducated, since many never have a chance to go to school in their entire life. Using any form of violence would destroy part of them, but the rest will show the worst kind of behavior in the future. I would recommend that they apply some techniques that could reverse not only their system, but could definitely change their mentality and their behavior. In doing so, they can become a nation with ethics, full morals, personality, and value. I certainly would encourage anyone who can bring peace to that nation, because I am part of that nation who was at one time suffering from all kinds of abuses at school.

I can certainly thank the United States not only for accepting me in its country as an immigrant, but for teaching me all the laws that exist in order to survive, which makes me a better American citizen. They have so much patience in the United States for training; they have been training me in a way to teach not only the people in my country, but to teach anyone about violence and crime around the world. I also thank the professors at the university for helping me on this entire project's research, because without all of those researchers, I probably would not know how to help those who are really in need of that kind of information.

In fact, coming from an area of abuse where there is only violence, it would be very hard not to be the worst criminal. I can sincerely say it was a miracle that I did not become a criminal, but I can say that it was luck to come here at an early age to learn not only the good way and good sense of humor, but to learn how anyone should live in a society. I always follow the law and the Bible, or I ask anyone what I should do so that I do not break any law. I believe in the law, respect, dignity, personality, morals, integrity, and values. I do not believe anyone in any country would be able to make it without those virtues.

Biography

Have we ever dreamed to be free from slavery? I fulfilled that dream. On the day that I made the decision to come to America, the Americans understood that I had left for a reason, and they did not ask me any questions about that decision until the present time. Today, I feel not only that I have to tell the truth, but to use this opportunity to thank them for all the help that I received from them. The day I came to America was July 1, 1982. It was my first day that I was free from abuse, and it was also the first day of my freedom.

In fact, I was born in the small land of Haiti, where I experienced hard times in the form of abusive treatment from the professors and my classmates. I finally made it to the end of my schooling, becoming a civil engineer. I requested a visa at the American Embassy, whose consulate favored me. When I arrived in America, it was a totally different history. I felt like there was a spray of love in the air that was touching my body; you could even smell and touch that love because it was so strong around me.

I am now not only free from abuse, but I have respect, peace, security, and all kinds of opportunities to become whatever I want. I live happily, and I am welcomed like others. I have never been mistreated by anyone and no one has ever discriminated against me. The Americans are always trying their best to help me in everything that I want to do.

By law, I had to have their high school diploma in order to register at college, so I finished both high school and colleges to get my degrees. Currently, I am attending Kaplan University to earn more degrees. The United States has been gracious to provide money for my school.

As of the writing of this book, I have worked as a health care administrator for many years in the United States. This has been my favorite job, because Americans have trained me to love everyone. In conclusion, the land of America is not only a land of opportunity, but simply a heaven land where citizens show love to each other.

References

Blakeslee, Sandra. (2007). "A Small Part of The Brain and Its Profound Effects." New York Times, February 6, 2007, 12-22.

Bostock, David:" *Aristotle's Ethics.* Oxford:" Oxford University Press, 2000.

Bovet Richard: "Carnival of Terror, page 127"

Bruskin & Goldring. (1993). America's number 1 fear: Public speaking. In Bruskin & Goldring (Eds.), Bruskin & Goldring report.

Callahan GN. Eating dirt. Emerg Infect Dis [serial online] 2003 Aug . Available from: URL: http://www.cdc.gov/ncidod/EID/vol9no8/03-0033.htm

Davis, Nick. "Haiti & Jamaica's Deadly Trade." Kingston, Jamaica: BBC News. October 25, 2008. Retrieved May 14, 2009. http://news.bbc.co.uk/1/hi/world/americas/7684983.stm. downbound.com. "Slavery." Retrieved May 14, 2009. http://www.downbound.com/Slavery_s/29.htm.

Dilworth, James (2008). On The Misrepresentation Of The Haitian Zombie. October, 9 2008.

Fagan Orla. "Violence and rape common in Haiti." Trocaire December 5, 2006.

Ginsburg Janet. (2005). Bacteria, viruses, and parasites may cause mental illness like depression, autism, and anorexia. Newsweek International December 1, 2005.

Goetz, M. J., et al.(1999). Criminality and Antisocial Behavior in Unselected Men with Sex Chromosome Abnormalities. *Psychological Medicine* 29 (July 1999): 953-62.

Jacobs, P. A. "Structural abnormalities of the sex chromosomes." *British Medical Bulletin*. 1969; 25: 94

Harvey, John A. and Barry E. Kosofsky, Eds. *Cocaine: Effects on the Developing Brain*. New York: Annals of the New York Academy of Sciences, 1998.

Harrington, Von Thomas. (2002-2004). Zombie Secrets p.1048.

Henry and Kwong, "Why is geophagy treated like dirt?", p. 366-368

Hooten, Thomas M. and Stuart B. Levy. (2001). Antimicrobial Resistance: A Plan of Action for Community Practice. *American Family Physician*, March 15, 2001. Retrieved May 14, 2009. http://www.aafp.org/afp/20010315/1087.html.

Jacobs, P. A. (1969). Structural abnormalities of the sex chromosomes. *British Medical Bulletin*. 1969; 25: 94

Kennedy, Robert. (1966). A *Speech on Race on October22,1966. Berkeley, California*.

Pearson, David. (2001). Combining energy drinks with alcohol potentially dangerous. Sciences Daily, November 14, 2001.

Pitt, John I. (1979). "Antibiotics kill your body's good bacteria too, leading to serious health risks, "Academy Press 1979.

Pitt, Rebecca. "Jean-Paul Sartre—Philosophy of Freedom" *Socialist Worker* Online, 11 June 2005. Retrieved May 14, 2009. www.socialistworker.co.uk/art.php?id=6657.

Quershi I. Adam. (2008). "RECOGNITION AND CONSEQUENCES OF OBSTRUCTIVE SLEEP APNEA HYPOPNEA SYNDROME. "*Otolaryngologic Clinics of North America*, Volume 32, Issue 2, Pages 303-331.S.Redline, K.Strohl March 11, 2008.

Robleto, Lizette. "True picture of HIV and AIDS in Haiti shows poverty and injustice biggest hurdle"January 29, 2008.

Rosenblum, David Felson. "Today News." February 10, 2009. "COHA ResearchAssociate.

Ruth, Joel A. (2009). WorldNetDaily.com on Voodoo and Clinton's fate Haitian sorcerers claim   credit   for his victories and defeats December 14, 1998.

Skinner, Benjamin. (2008). Author Struggles to Stay Removed from Slave Trade. Politics and Societies. March 11, 2008..

Silvestre, Emmanuel, Jaime Rijo, and Huberto Bogaert, *La Neo-Prostitución Infantil en República Dominicana*, UNICEF and ONAPLAN, 1999, 33.

Steen, R. Grant. *DNA and Destiny, Nature & Nurture in Human Behavior.* New York: Plenum Press, 1996.

Stone, Richard and Katrina Kelner. "Violence: No Silver Bullet: Introduction to Special Issue on Violence." *Science,* July 28, 2000. Retrieved May 14, 2009. http://www.sciencemag.org/cgi/content/summary/289/5479/569.

Taylor, Lawrence. Born *to Crime, The Genetic Causes of Criminal Behavior.* Connecticut: Greenwood Press, 1984.

Theilgaard, Alice. "A Psychological Study of the Personalities of XYY and XXY Men." *Acta Psychiatrica Scandinavica* 69 (Suppl. 315) (1984).

U.S. Department of State, *Country Reports—2003: Dominican Republic,* Sections 5 and 6c.

Vestal, Theodore. (2001). "Delivered at an Evening of Celebration and Remembrance of the 40th Anniversary of the Founding of the Peace Corps." Tulsa, Oklahoma April 28, 2001.

Vitanza, S., Vogel, L.C., & Marshall, L.L. (1995). Distress and symptoms of posttraumatic stress disorder in abused women. Violence and Victims, 10, 23-34.

Wassenaar, Trudy M. "Bacteria: More than Pathogens." actionbioscience. org. Retrieved May 14, 2009. http://www.actionbioscience.org/biodiversity/wassenaar.html.

Williams, Carol J. (2003). "Official recognition of voodoo in Haiti stirs enthusiasm, concern." Los Angeles Times, 6 Aug 2003.

WINERMAN LEA. Criminal profiling: the reality behind the myth. APA Monitor article, page 66 (July/*August 2004*)

Yasumoto T, Kao CY: Tetradotoxin and the Haitian zombie. Toxicon 1986; 24:747-749.

From the CDC. Tetradotoxin poisoning associated with pufferfish transported from Japan. JAMA 1996; 275:1931

American Psychological Association. "Psychology and Law Enforcement—Criminal Profiling." Retrieved April 27, 2007, from http://www.apahelpcenter.org/articles/article.php?id=64, 2004.

American Psychiatric Association. "Diagnostic and Statistical Manual of Mental Disorders: DSM-IV. "American Psychiatric Pub., Inc. 1994. (Feb. 28, 2008) http://books.google.com/books?id=3SQrtpnH b9MC&printsec=frontcover& dq=dsm-iv&source= gbs summary.r

Ball State University:" Combining Energy Drinks with Alcohol Potentially Dangerous" *Science Daily*, November 16, 2001. Retrieved April 21, 2009, from http://www.sciencedaily.com/releases/2001/11/011116065754.htm

Clark County (IN) Prosecuting Attorney, The. "Domestic Violence." Retrieved from Google Cache (May 10, 2009) May 14, 2009. http://www.clarkprosecutor.org/html/domviol/effects.htm (enter URL in Google Search).

Cleveland Clinic Foundation, The. "Bacterial vs Viral/Respiratory Tract Infections." Retrieved on May 14, 2009. http://my.clevelandclinic.org/disorders/bronchitis/hic_bacterial_vs_viral-respiratory_tract_infections.aspx.

Earthlife.net. "Bacteria and Disease." Retrieved May 14, 2009.

http://www.earthlife.net/prokaryotes/disease.html.

Haiti makes voodoo official | Voodoo has been practiced in Haiti since the late 18th Century, but only now has it been recognized as a religion on a par with others worshipped in the country—BBC (Apr. 30, 2003).

Insuring America's Health: "Principles and Recommendations, Institute of Medicine at the National Academies of Science," 2004-01-14

Rosenblum, David Felson. "TodayNews" February10,2009. COHA Research Associate.

Ruth, Joel A. 2009 WorldNetDaily.com on (Voodoo and Clinton's fate Haitian sorcerers claim credit for his victories and defeats December 14, 1998).

LSU Law Center. "Food Sanitation." Medical and Public Health Law Site. Retrieved May 14, 2009. http://biotech.law.lsu.edu/books/lbb/x582.htm.

Medical News Today. "Children Prone to Ear Infections Have High Rates of Disease Producing Bacteria." Retrieved May 14, 2009. http://www.medicalnewstoday.com/articles/26631.php.

MEDICC Review is a quarterly on-line publication of Medical Education Cooperation with Cuba.

MEDICC, 328 Flatbush Ave... Box 406, Brooklyn, NY 11238. Please address all correspondence to medic@informed.sld.cu

National Public Radio. "Author Struggles to Stay Removed from Slave Trade." Review of Benjamin Skinner's *A Crime So Monstrous: Face-to-Face with Modern-Day Slavery.* NPR.org, March 11, 2008. Retrieved May 14, 2009. http://www.npr.org/templates/story/story.php?storyId=88102060.

Online Resource Centre. "Water Sanitation." Retrieved May 14, 2009. http://nposonline.net/water-sanitation.shtml.

Violence. (2009). *Science,* July 28, 2000. Retrieved May 14, 2009. U.S. Department of State, *Country Reports—2003: Dominican Republic,* Sections 5 and 6c.